Hilarie Wakefield Dayton

Sew Bags

The Practical Guide to Making Purses, Totes, Clutches & More

13 SKILL-BUILDING PROJECTS

stashBOOKS.

an imprint of C&T Publishing

Text and artwork copyright © 2019 by HILARIE WAKEFIELD DAYTON

Photography and artwork copyright © 2019 by C&T Publishing, Inc.

Publisher: AMY MARSON

Creative Director: GAILEN RUNGE

Acquisitions Editor: ROXANE CERDA

Managing Editor: LIZ ANELOSKI

Editor: BETH BAUMGARTEL

Technical Editor: DEBBIE RODGERS

Cover/Book Designer: APRIL MOSTEK

Production Coordinator: ZINNIA HEINZMANN

Production Editor: JENNIFER WARREN

Illustrators: LINDA JOHNSON and HILARIE WAKEFIELD DAYTON

Photo Assistant: RACHEL HOLMES

Cover photography by KELLY BURGOYNE of C&T Publishing, Inc.

Interior photography by KELLY BURGOYNE of C&T Publishing, Inc., unless otherwise noted

Published by Stash Books, an imprint of C&T Publishing, Inc., P.O. Box 1456, Lafayette, CA 94549

Library of Congress Cataloging-in-Publication Data

Names: Dayton, Hilarie Wakefield, author.

Title: Sew bags : the practical guide to making purses, totes, clutches & more, 13 skill-building projects / Hilarie Wakefield Dayton.

Description: Lafayette, CA : C&T Publishing, Inc., [2019]

Identifiers: LCCN 2018037405 | ISBN 9781617457913 (softcover)

Subjects: LCSH: Tote bags. | Handbags. | Sewing.

Classification: LCC TT667 .D356 2019 | DDC 646.4/8--dc23

LC record available at https://lccn.loc.gov/2018037405

Printed in China

10 9 8 7 6 5 4 3 2 1

Dedication

To my children, Christopher and Caroline. I hope that you find a special something in life that brings joy and meaning to you. Stick with it and with each other.

To my dear husband, David, who is (mostly) nothing but encouraging and supportive (and hot!).

Acknowledgments

In a sense, I have been working on this book over the course of my entire lifetime. I learned to sew as a very young child, and there has never been a time when I haven't been learning how to make something. Over the years, I have learned from books, teachers, friends, professors, and a strong curiosity about how clothes were made—I loved taking clothes apart and sewing them back together. Without the encouragement of friends and family, however, this book would have never been written.

Sewing is my lifelong love and passion; I want to share it with you. I opened Little Stitch Studio with this sentiment in mind and a determination to share my love of fashion, sewing, and design with kids (and adults) of all ages.

Thank you to all the students that I have had the good fortune to share time sewing, laughing, and learning with each week. My appreciation goes to all the parents for their support and enthusiasm.

My sincere thanks to Annabel for inviting me to collaborate on some projects with her and for believing in me. Without her support, I would have never had the confidence to put pen to paper.

Finally, my gratitude to the staff at C&T Publishing—most notably Roxane and Liz—for taking a chance on me and for their enduring patience. Without the extensive knowledge, wit, and intelligence of my editor, Beth, this book would not have come together.

Thank you, *Hilarie XO*

Contents

Welcome

For Adult Sewists

This book is meant to be a beginning, an invitation to learn to sew. It happens to be about making handbags; however, the skills you will learn are infinitely adaptable. The very same sewing skills used to make all kinds of handbags are also used to make pillows, clothing, soft toys, and curtains. Master the fundamental building blocks of sewing demonstrated in the pages of this book, and they will forever be a part of your repertoire.

I hope to teach you how to sew in such a way that is not so much about following the instructions as it is about becoming a more skilled and thoughtful sewist. You will learn how a handbag is built and how to plan, choose fabrics, use patterns, pin, hand and machine stitch, embellish, and much more. I also hope to teach you about design, about the relationship between line and shape. With a basic understanding of construction, the logic about turning flat fabric into all kinds of handbags becomes considerably clearer.

My design formula starts with essential handbag shapes and injects them with style. My bags don't necessarily cater to seasonal trends but flow from season to season. Every season, we all seem to end up in a quandary over which handbag to carry, and we often compromise on shape, size, color, or even strap length. If you are shopping for a new bag, cost is an additional consideration. You don't have to compromise when you are the designer because you can make the bag of your dreams.

I welcome you to explore the pages of this book. Gain insight into the design process and learn the sewing techniques to develop your own amazing bags!

For Kid Sewists

Are you obsessed with fashion and sewing? I'll bet you are! In this book, we are going to have a lot of fun exploring cool sewing techniques, and you will get to make lots of special projects. I'll show you how to combine colors, fabrics, and trims. You will learn how to use a pattern and make some pretty fabulous handbags.

I remember as a young girl wanting to make beautiful clothes, accessories, and stuff for my room but not knowing where to begin. It was so frustrating! At that time, all the sewing books were for grown-ups, and the sewing patterns left me feeling uninspired. I would have loved to have a book like *Sew Bags* to show me that even though something may look tricky to sew, it's really very easy once you get the hang of using a sewing machine. The key is to start with simple shapes that are endlessly versatile and are just begging for your personal touch. If you can sew a straight line, you can make these projects!

Today, you have so many options for design ideas: blogs, Pinterest, books, magazines, and YouTube. Unfortunately, all this creative inspiration may also leave you feeling drained or inadequate. I know what it's like when your ideas greatly outpace your skills. I am here to help you learn and build on the sewing skills that you already have and to show you new techniques so that you can find your design voice and go for it!

You will be amazed by the bags you can make. Nothing in this book is too complicated! If you don't understand a step or you need help, ask an adult. Everybody needs help at some point, so don't be shy about asking. Cutting, sewing, pressing, and reading patterns are all skills that take time and patience to develop.

I encourage you to really take your time learning these new steps and to practice them. Once you've given a project a try, experiment and see what other ways you change it up to make it your own. Try making it bigger or smaller, or mix and match the fabrics and trims. There so many design options for you.

In my classroom at Little Stitch Studio, we have a bin full of scraps. I recommend that you keep all your fabric scraps. (You can ask if your fabric store has end cuts for discounted prices or cut up old clothes, sheets, and curtains to make your own scrap bin.) When you want to practice techniques or want a small side project to work on, grab fabric from the scrap bin and whip up some sewing magic! Open-ended sewing with scraps seems to take the quest for perfection out of the equation. Every day I see kids just like you learn how to use the fabric and materials in a fun, no-pressure way. Later, that scrap-sewing practice gives you the finesse to create more elaborate projects.

Maybe you dream of being a fashion designer, or maybe you just want to have fun making things for yourself and your friends. Whatever your wishes, *Sew Bags* is your guide to making your creative dreams come true.

How to Think like a Designer

Inspiration

What inspires you? To me, inspiration is a magical type of feeling—a feeling in which you might hear your mind thinking as it forms a picture. How do you capture this magic? Where do ideas come from? I find inspiration from running, showering, sleeping, a quiet space, music … boredom. Yes, that's right. *Boredom!* Let your mind wander. Daydream, turn off your phone, sit, play, doodle, and even work on some mind-numbing task. I find that when I clear my head, my brain comes up with some pretty brilliant stuff. That's where the idea for this book came from!

Start by keeping a sketchbook or journal where you can record little flashes and inspirations that come to your intuitive mind when you least expect them. This practice prevents you from forgetting ideas and allows you to look at them later. It also gets your positive energy flowing and automatically helps you open up to your creativity. Bring your sketchbook with you wherever you go. At night, when my mind is racing, I jot down ideas for new projects and details about old projects. Just a quick sketch or phrase or list of colors is all it takes to hold me over. These reminders ease the anxiety that if I don't make notes when I get a design flash, I'll forget that moment of brilliance.

Creativity comes from making unusual connections, so make creative thinking a habit. Through consistent practice, you will build your creative muscle. Practice frees our minds to unveil great ideas. If you are like me, you don't enjoy creating something that isn't fantastic. It's easy to start judging your work and convince yourself that your ideas aren't good enough. Give yourself permission to fail; it is all part of the journey to focus your energy and ideas.

Visualization Exercise

I want you to build a collection of visual elements that will help you create a central design idea or theme. Begin by gathering things you are drawn to: colors, fabric, pictures, clothes, art. Find a table or shelf and arrange a vignette with these items. By looking at them from different angles, moving them around, and mixing the different items, your design ideas will start to take shape. Step away. Go do something else that excites you. Let your mind wander. As your ideas return, listen to your inner designer to affirm that you are on the right path. This will help you find your authentic self.

Don't take the process too seriously, and don't worry if you feel like you don't have any ideas. They will come!

Mood Boards

Mood boards are the perfect playground for Inspiration and exploration. Start saving things that speak to you and display them on poster board to create a vision of your world. Collect illustrations, magazine pages, paint chips, photos, all kinds of fabric swatches and other textures, ribbons, trims, yarn, graphic patterns, art, words, and affirmations. If this collection process sounds a lot like the creative visualization exercise, that's because it is. It is so fun and important to gather visual tokens of the things that excite you. The process is collective and helps to tell the whole story.

A mood board serves as a sort of treasure map. It is a tangible picture of your aspirations and vision. Creativity also comes with the need to edit! You might have a difficult time editing because all your ideas are so compelling and beguiling; however, to be a good designer you also need to learn to be a good editor. This exercise helps you learn to extract the essence of the style ideas that draw you in. When choosing items to collect for your mood board, ask yourself, "How will I use my bag?" "What colors speak to me?" "How do I want to feel?"

You can make mood boards for anything—room decor, garden plans, back-to-school shopping, and even color palettes. You only need your inspirational collection and a few other things you can probably find around the house.

Here is what you will need:

- Inspirational materials
- Poster board (I like to cut the big boards in half for two boards 14″ × 22″.)
- Markers
- Glue
- Tape
- Scissors

Have fun with it, because it's all about you!

Color

Color creates focal points and adds personality to a design. Color choice is personal, but there are some things you should know so you can use color to create designs as unique as you are.

Using a color wheel and knowing terms like *primary*, *complementary*, *warm*, *cool*, *hue*, and *tint* are important to understanding the power of color.

There are a few color schemes that are used in design work, but you should know a few things first:

Primary colors (red, yellow, and blue) cannot be created by mixing any other colors.

Secondary colors (orange, green, and violet) are created by mixing two primary colors together.

Tertiary colors are created by mixing one primary and one secondary color together.

A **tint** is the combination of a primary, secondary, or tertiary color with white.

A **tone** is created by combining a primary, secondary, or tertiary color with gray.

A **shade** is the combination of a primary, secondary, or tertiary color with black.

A **hue** is like a last name; it refers to the dominant color family of any particular color.

Warm colors are reds, oranges, and yellows.

Cool colors are blues, greens, and purples.

You can create color schemes by combining colors in specific ways.

A **complementary color scheme** combines colors that appear opposite of each other on the color wheel, like blue and orange.

A **monochromatic color scheme** uses the tints, tones, and shades of a single hue.

An **analogous color scheme** employs a continuous relationship within 90° of each color on the color wheel (three colors next to each other on the color wheel).

Color Is Complex!

Neutral Colors

Neutral colors, also referred to as *earth tones*, appear to be without color and aren't represented on a color wheel. They can be created by mixing two complementary colors or by combining a pure color with white, black, or gray. **Pure neutral colors** include black, white, and all grays, while **near neutrals** include browns, tans, and darker colors. Since these colors are created by mixing other colors, however, they will contain some undertone.

Mass Tone and Undertone

Color, when mixed, may have a slightly heavier dose of either a red or orange tone, making it warm, or have a hint of blue or purple, making it cool. To understand undertone, you need to know that colors have both a *mass tone* and an *undertone*. **Mass tone** is the color that you identify first, like red or blue. The **undertone** is a bit more subjective and influenced by light and surrounding colors.

Undertones become more apparent when they are used in combination with other colors. In some colors, the mass tone and undertone are very similar; other colors have undertones that are quite different from their mass tone. Ultimately, the fact that it does contain some undertone will result in more contrast when paired with stronger hues.

Color Scale Exercise

Play with watercolors, crayons, markers, chalk, or any form of color to see how you can mix colors and create unlimited variations of your favorites. You might want to keep a notebook. Color your world!

1. Start with primary colors and add varying amounts of white, gray, and black.

2. Make secondary colors by mixing 2 primary colors.

3. Make tertiary colors by mixing 1 primary and 1 secondary color.

4. Add white, gray, and black to any and every color!

The Design Process

Now you get to put your inspiration to work and get started on the design process! It's important to consider the elements of design, scale, and proportion and then translate those elements into rough sketches of your visions.

Proportion, Scale, and Harmony

When color, line, shape, and texture are all in balance, the design is considered *harmonious*. One of the first things you learn about illustrating is that the human body is generally drawn so it is the equivalent of eight heads tall. In fashion illustration, however, the body is elongated to better show the clothes. Instead of being eight heads tall, the body is *nine* heads tall.

Proportion is an element of design that pertains to how two objects relate or look together. For example, a long shirt looks different on children of differing heights. On one child it looks fantastic, and on the other it is overwhelming. The proportion of the shirt (or the size of the shirt in relation to the size of the child) just looks wrong. You'll start to notice when the proportions in nature, on people, and maybe even on a handbag look great or not so great.

For a designer, it is difficult to explain when a design or outfit is in proportion. That sense of what looks good and what doesn't is referred to as having "an eye for design." Since there is no right or wrong answer, proportion is in the eye of the designer. See The Rule of Thirds (next page) to better understand proportion.

Scale refers to the relationship between two or more objects, one of which is a common standard (for example, a human body). In design, when we talk about scale, we are usually talking about the quality of size in comparison to something else. It creates perspective and, as a design element, provides designers with endless options for variation.

Scale is absolute; proportion is relative. One way to think about scale is to consider the size of a print or motif on a piece of fabric. For example, larger bags that don't have a lot of seams look great in large prints, but a large print or motif might be chopped off by the seams or size of a small bag. A small print is perfect for any size bag. As a designer, you will want to consider the size and scale of the fabric pattern for your handbag design.

Harmony is the balance of design elements. This happens when color, pattern, texture, proportion, and scale are in concert and the design looks great. No one part is more important than the whole design.

The Rule of Thirds

Much of what we consider beautiful in this world is based on proportion. The golden ratio of dividing things into thirds is like having the perfect design tool and the perfect starting point for designing.

Start by dividing the handbag (or whatever you are designing) into three equal parts. Those dividing lines are where your focal points should be. The rule of thirds is a simplified concept rooted in mathematics, and it lends balance to a design while making it more interesting and engaging to the eye. This design rule brings separate elements together to form a whole. By positioning lines and shapes in certain ways, you can control where the eye goes. Naturally, you want the eye to first land on the main focal point, but then where does it go? Good design directs the eye to the focal point and then the rest of the bag (or garment).

Sketching

This is your opportunity to showcase your creative vision. Sketching is a great way to explore and test ideas before investing too much time. Beautiful fashion sketches are often shown as part of the glamorized process of fashion design. While it can be fun to illustrate an idea on paper, it can be harder to turn that sketch into an actual bag. The trick is to consider function while retaining the feeling of the original idea. As a designer, the way you actively draw or illustrate your designs can be highly influential in the actual designs you create, as you translate your sketches into designs. Feel free to add to your drawing with colored pencils or watercolors!

Here are a few exercises to help you practice your sketching talents. The more you sketch, the better your drawings become!

- Draw a bag for an acrobat.

- What kind of bag would suit a young girl?

- Draw a cross body bag on a person so their hands are free.

- Draw a bag with lots of bright colors.

- Add an appliqué on any bag you already drew.

- How about drawing the inside of a bag, especially with a few pockets?

- Show how a bag closes.

- Draw a bag for a teenager; then draw a bag for a mom. Note how they are different.

- Don't forget to draw some wristlets and even some wallets!

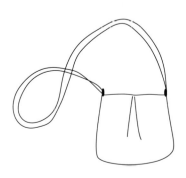

Building Blocks

Once you understand a bit about patterns and fabrics, the rest is easy. Choosing the best fabric is important, and deciding whether you want to add interfacing is fundamental. All that information is right here. Get ready to be inspired!

How Patterns Work

Understanding a pattern and how it works is key to expanding your sewing knowledge. If you haven't used a pattern before, don't worry! The secret is to take your time reading and understanding the pattern and then to follow the step-by-step instructions and photographs.

A pattern is used to make a template for each part of the bag (such as the front, back, flap, or strap). Each piece is laid on top of fabric and cut out so that the fabric matches the pattern shape.

Each pattern piece is framed by a solid outline, representing the cut line. Other markings tell you how to add shape and other design elements. The patterns can be reused to produce the same designs again and again. They can also include important information on how to match pieces together and how many pieces to cut.

Sewing handbags is a logical process. Each seam or stitching line exists for an important reason; they help shape the cloth and reinforce it for strength. Once you grasp the relationship between the pattern and the sewing steps, the process is easy. The logic of what you are doing and why you need to put two pieces of shaped fabric together in a specific order becomes clear.

Think of a pattern as a two-dimensional jigsaw puzzle that, once constructed, turns into a three-dimensional object. Picturing fabric pieces this way helps you see what a pattern piece should look like and how it fits into the finished object.

Sometimes the patterns are so simple that I provide the measurements. In these cases, draw the square or rectangular pattern directly on the fabric with tailor's chalk or a fabric-marking pen. If you prefer, draw the measurements on paper to make your own pattern.

Pattern Talk

Pattern markings include a group of symbols and instructions for how to lay out, fold, cut, and shape your fabric into the handbag or whatever you are making. The same markings that are found on patterns for a simple project, such as a tote bag, are the same ones found on a much more complicated wedding dress. When you build skills with each project, you gain a better understanding of the process. You will be able to make anything!

Pattern Markings

Learning to read a pattern and understanding the symbols is kind of like learning another language—but an easy language!

Cutting line   The cutting line is the pattern "frame," or outside line, that represents the line on which to cut.

Place on fabric fold line   This line indicates that you need to fold the fabric in half and align the fold line on the pattern with the folded edge of the fabric. This pattern represents only half of the whole handbag piece. By placing the pattern on the fabric fold and cutting it out as directed, you end up with one full-size piece of fabric with symmetrical left and right sides.

Dashed interior fold lines   These lines are found within the outside cutting lines of the pattern and indicate where you will need to fold the fabric during construction to make pockets, pleats, and hems.

Grainline   This is a line in the center of the pattern, marked with an arrow at each end. It indicates how to position the pattern on the fabric so the fabric will be cut on the straight grain. The straight grainline is parallel to the selvage (finished edge).

Label   The pattern label indicates the name of the part that you are cutting (for example, "Purse Flap"), as well as how many times you need to cut it out and whether you need to cut lining fabric or interfacing, too.

Seam allowance   Seam allowance is often indicated in the sewing instructions instead of directly on the pattern. It is the margin of space between the cutting line and sewing line. If you don't sew with the indicated seam allowance, your bag might be larger or smaller than

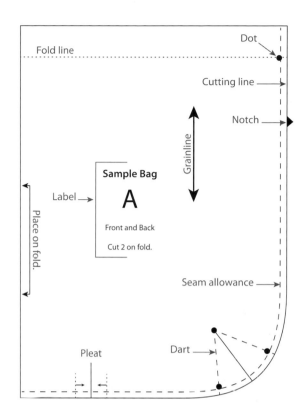

designed. All of the projects in this book have a ½˝ seam allowance unless otherwise specified.

Notch   A notch is a pattern marking that shows you where to join two pieces of fabric. You will want to copy the notch from the pattern to the cut fabric pieces so that they can be sewn together correctly. Simple patterns, like the ones included in this book, don't often need notches, so don't worry if you don't see any!

Dots   Dots indicate the starting and stopping points for stitching or matching up points. You will find dots also used to indicate strap placements.

Darts   Darts add shape and fullness. They are formed by pinching a small triangle out of a flat piece of fabric.

Pleat   Pleats create additional volume in a small space. They are formed by folding the fabric and stitching it as indicated.

Mini-Pattern Exercise

In my classes, kids are always taking pieces of fabric and wrapping, tucking, and tying them around themselves in their efforts to design dresses or costumes. These experiments are a great way to learn how fabric drapes. I always encourage them to keep experimenting.

In fashion design, there are two main ways to develop a garment. The first is through the flat pattern, which we will be doing in this book. As we discussed earlier in this chapter, flat pattern pieces can be manipulated into curved shapes through cutting and sewing shaped pieces of fabric and with darts and pleats. However, draping is a different design method. It is the act draping fabric on a dress form and then transforming the shaped pieces into flat patterns. I encourage you to learn more about both methods and try them for yourself.

We are going to concentrate on using flat patterns, and the best way to learn is by practice. To illustrate the basic pattern

principles, I have the kids in my class do this fun paper purse exercise. This exercise is also a great way to test your own designs on paper before you sew them up in fabric.

You'll need craft papers (or wrapping paper), scissors, a transparent ruler, a marking pen, tape, and the Mini-Pattern Exercise patterns (next page). These patterns are scaled to fit a posable drawing figure or Barbie doll.

1. Trace the pattern shapes and cut them out. Copy the marking guides, too (we discussed these in Pattern Talk, page 14).

2. The interior dashed lines show you how to fold the paper.

3. The outside cutting lines indicate where to tape the paper together to create the little paper handbags.

4. After assembling your bags, consider adding stickers, beads, and ribbon to further bring your vision to life.

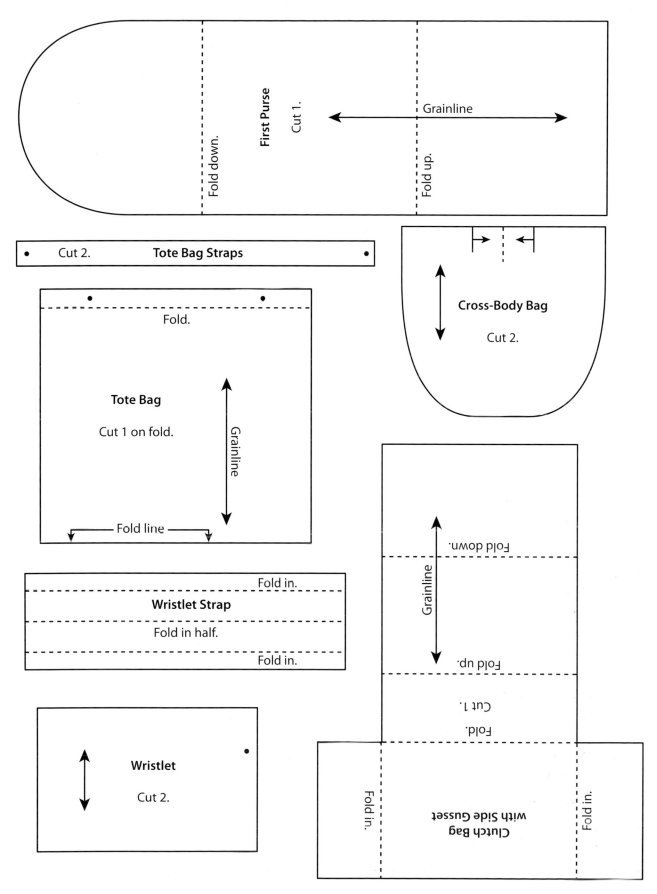

First Purse

Cut 1.

Fold down.

Grainline

Fold up.

Cut 2. **Tote Bag Straps**

Cross-Body Bag

Cut 2.

Fold.

Tote Bag

Cut 1 on fold.

Grainline

Fold line

Grainline

Fold down.

Fold up.

Cut 1.

Fold.

Fold in. **Wristlet Strap**

Fold in half.

Fold in.

Fold in.

Fold in.

Clutch Bag with Side Gusset

Wristlet

Cut 2.

Pattern Instructions

To use the full-size patterns provided, you need to copy the patterns onto pattern or craft paper so you can use them over and over again. You also need to copy the markings onto the paper patterns (see Pattern Markings, page 15).

Positioning the Patterns on the Fabric

Before you lay out the patterns on the fabric, it is a good idea to press out any creases in your fabric. You will want to get the fabric nice and smooth to ensure an accurate and precise cut. For making purses, I do not recommend prewashing the fabric. Unwashed fabric has a stiffer body that will lend a better shape to the finished bag.

1. Use paper scissors to cut out your patterns.

2. Determine if you need to cut the pieces from a single or double layer of fabric or if you need to place the pattern on the fabric fold. Each pattern piece specifies how many pieces of fabric need to be cut. The cutting instructions for each project will also let you know how to cut your fabric.

3. Fold the fabric in half, right sides together, if the pieces are to be cut twice. Lay out the pattern pieces and be sure to notice if any patterns need to be aligned with the fabric fold.

4. Pin each pattern to the fabric, smoothing the fabric as you go, and place the pins within the seam allowance to avoid damaging the fabric that will make up the bag. Make sure the grain-line marking runs parallel to the fabric selvage.

5. Use your fabric scissors to cut out the fabric along the pattern cutting lines.

6. Transfer all pattern markings (next page) before removing the pattern pieces.

Tip

If you have two pieces that need to be cut on the fold, you might want to fold each selvage in toward the center of the fabric so you have two fabric folds.

Tip

The selvage is the "self edge," the finished woven strip on both sides of the fabric. It prevents the fabric from raveling and fraying, but it is not good to use for sewing. Be sure to place the patterns at least ½″ away from the selvage.

Transferring Pattern Markings

There are several methods for transferring pattern markings to fabric. Water-soluble markers, tailor's chalk, and chalk pencils are my methods of choice. Keep in mind that the markings help to line up each pattern piece, so taking the time to properly mark your pattern will go a long way toward creating a satisfying bag that will make you proud. Always mark the fabric with the necessary pattern markings before removing the pattern; this ensures accurate marking. Start transferring the markings from the pattern to the fabric at the outside edges and then work toward the center. Unless otherwise stated, copy the markings onto the wrong side of the fabric. Easy, right? Let's do it!

Working with one piece at a time, carefully remove just enough pins so that you can mark the fabric. If you are drawing a line, use a straight-edge ruler as a guide. If there is an additional fabric layer, mark that separately.

Mark a dot: Use a straight pin to pierce the pattern piece and fabric right through the center of the dot. Carefully lift the pattern paper (while still holding the pinned fabric in place) and mark the fabric with tailor's chalk or a fabric-marking pen. Repeat on the next layer of fabric. Repeat for each dot.

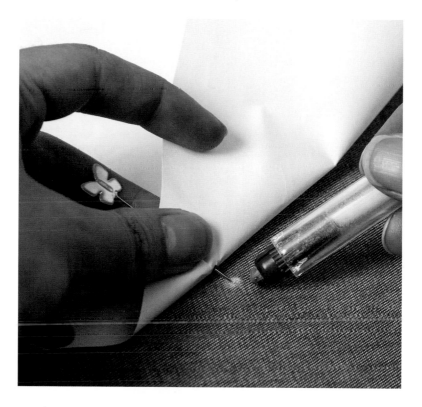

Mark an interior fold line (for a pocket): With the pocket facing down, fold back the pattern along the interior fold line and mark the fabric along the fold of the pattern.

Mark start/stop stitching lines: Sometimes there are vertical lines instead of dots on the patterns to indicate where to fold for a pleat or where to start and stop stitching when you need to leave an opening in a seam. Mark these just like the dots.

Fabric and Fibers

Fabrics are made from various materials (fibers) that are available from nature, like cotton and silk. They are chemically manufactured (like polyester) or made from a mix of natural and synthetic materials. Fabrics are classified based on the origin of the fiber and its finishing process. Basically, fabrics are woven and don't stretch *or* they are knit and do stretch! I made all the handbags featured in this book from woven fabrics.

Types of Fabric Fibers

Natural Fibers

Natural fabrics are those created from the fibers of animal coats, plants, leaves, and stems. The fabrics breathe and are absorbent, soft, and durable.

Cotton is grown from seeds and is unquestioningly the most widely used natural fiber.

Linen is the world's strongest natural fiber. Linen cloth is made from flax; the fibers are generally longer than cotton fibers, adding strength and texture to the finished fabric.

Silk is luxurious and favored by high-fashion devotees. It is created by silk worms.

Wool is a fiber derived from the undercoat of animals such as sheep, goats, rabbits, and camels. The hair is cleaned, combed, and woven or knitted into fabric. It is extra warm, durable, moisture-absorbent, and versatile.

Man-Made Fibers

Synthetic or man-made fabrics are made from fibers that are either completely inorganic materials or a blend of inorganic and natural fibers, combined with chemicals through complex processing. These fibers produce fabrics with a variety of properties such as strength, sheen, and stretch. They are also frequently resistant to shrinking and tend to dry quickly.

Types of Fabric Construction

Fabric is further classified by structure. The fibers described at the left are made into yarns, which are used to weave or knit fabrics.

Woven fabric consists of two sets of yarns woven at right angles to each other. This structure provides a sturdy fabric with little to no stretch.

Knit fabrics have intersecting loops of yarn knitted on a machine. They stretch and do not ravel. They take on the shape of the wearer.

Nonwoven fabrics are felted or pressed, depending on the natural ability of the fibers to shrink. They are not as sturdy or durable as other fabrics, but they are tactile and fun to work with.

Fabric Characteristics

Grain refers to how the threads are woven: They are either vertical (parallel to the selvage) or horizontal (perpendicular to the selvage). The vertical grain, called the **warp grain** or **straight grain**, are the strongest threads, so most fabrics are cut so that the pattern pieces are aligned with the straight grain. The horizontal threads are called the **weft grain**. The warp and weft grains don't stretch; however, many fabrics stretch on the **bias grain**, which is a 45° angle between the warp and weft grains.

A fabric's **weight** is determined by the weaving method and the fiber. For instance, chiffon is very lightweight because it is loosely woven, whereas canvas is heavyweight because of its twill weave and heavier cotton fabric. Fabric weight is particularly important when choosing between two similar fabrics with different weights. The most appropriate fabric weight usually depends on the end use of whatever you are making. Handbags usually benefit from fabric that is medium-weight to heavyweight—if you love a lightweight fabric, however, you can add interfacing and fusible fleece to make it heavier. Typical fabric weights are classified as decorator, quilt weight, and garment weight (lightweight, medium-weight, and heavyweight). The handbags in this book were made from a variety of fabric weights.

The **drape** of a fabric refers to the way it hangs or clings to the body. If the fabric is fluid and drapes in beautiful folds, it is considered to have **high drape**. Silk, satin, and chiffon have high drape. Fabric that is more rigid or stiff, such as denim or corduroy, has a **low drape**. When you are choosing fabric for your handbags, the outer fabric needs to have a low drape, whereas the lining would look elegant if it had more drape.

The **hand** of fabric simply refers to how it feels against your skin. It describes the tactile quality of the fabric. Does it feel soft? Crisp? Silky? The way the fabric feels contributes to the overall use and look of the finished design.

Fabric **nap** refers to raised surface texture, like what you feel on velvet, corduroy, and fur. You can feel the nap when you run your hand over the fabric and even see the subtle color change when you rub the fabric against the nap. The fibers or hair on napped fabrics all lay in one direction, so if you choose a fabric with a nap, you need to make sure all the pattern pieces are positioned in the same direction on the fabric.

Lining, Interfacing, and Fusible Fleece

Most of your sewing—whether to make handbags, pillows, clothing, or almost anything else—will require lining, interfacing, and sometimes fusible fleece for extra stability.

Lining

Lining shouldn't be an afterthought—it is an integral part of your project. Use it to your advantage and make it bright and fun. When you reach in your handbag to get your keys, you'll smile!

A **lining** is a separate layer of fabric sewn inside of a bag or garment. It hides raw edges, internal seams, and darts. The lining provides a clean finish, adds structure and a bit of reinforcement, and can hold pockets or dividers.

Suitable lining fabric comes in many colors and patterns. You can choose a color that matches the bag fabric or even a fun contrasting color. When you are choosing lining fabric, make sure that its washing care requirements are compatible with the outside bag fabric. Good options for lining fabrics include cotton and silk. In general, you want the lining fabric to be a lighter weight than your fashion fabric and light enough in color that it doesn't show through.

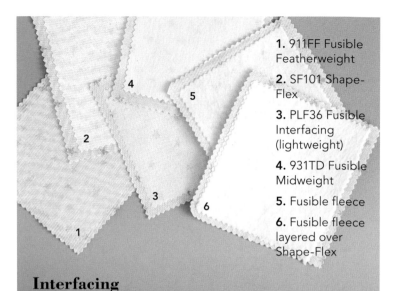

1. 911FF Fusible Featherweight
2. SF101 Shape-Flex
3. PLF36 Fusible Interfacing (lightweight)
4. 931TD Fusible Midweight
5. Fusible fleece
6. Fusible fleece layered over Shape-Flex

Interfacing

Interfacing is an important component in the construction of handbags. It strengthens and stabilizes the fabric while preventing it from distorting or stretching out of shape, and adds support and structure to the bag. I prefer fusible interfacing for its ease and flexibility. Most fusible interfacings are *nonwoven*, which means they don't have a grain, they will stretch with the fabric, and you can cut them out without worrying about grainline. Plus, for the longer straps, you can cut two or more pieces to make up the full length. Just overlap them ⅛″ or so when fusing to the fabric.

I used Pellon SF101 Shape-Flex to make the handbags in this book.

> **Tip**
> *The steps and pattern pieces to make the lining are the same as for the outside of the bag.*

> **Tip**
> *When cutting interfacing for a specific pattern piece, make sure the interfacing is cut so that it is approximately ⅜″–½″ smaller than the fabric on all sides. This will help to reduce bulk along the seamlines.*

Fusible fleece

Fusible fleece is unparalleled in adding support and a bit of loft (a thin layer of padding) to a bag or other project. Sometimes a fabric needs a bit more than interfacing, so I fuse a layer of fusible fleece on top of the interfacing to add substantial body to the fabric (see item 6 in Interfacing, previous page). It's your choice!

Shopping for Fabric

Before shopping for fabric, have a plan! Consider the overall design, function, and look of the bag you plan to make first before heading to the fabric store or looking online. Remember to look at your mood board for color, pattern, and texture inspiration. Review the bags in this book to see how the fabric choice makes them all look so different.

Local fabric stores and online shops are great places to visit; however, you can find awesome fabrics by refashioning or upcycling your own clothes and bags or those from a thrift store. Think about all the fabric and textiles that are already in your own home: curtains, shower curtains, outgrown sweaters (perfect for felting!). The only limits are your imagination.

Local fabric stores or national chain stores generally have a wide selection and will often cut a swatch for you to consider (or add to your mood board). With their hundreds of options and rows upon rows of fabric bolts, these stores can be inspiring and overwhelming. Sometimes you will have to shop around to get the perfect fabric. While nothing beats spending an afternoon in a fabric store and touching all those lovely fabrics, there are vast amounts of different fabrics available online. Online stores usually have some great deals, free shipping, and fabrics organized by designer, theme, manufacturer, or color. Online stores will frequently offer swatches, as well.

Shopping for Handbag Fabrics, Linings, and Interfacings

Unless otherwise stated, I recommend using the following fashion fabrics for the bag exterior, lining, and interfacing (and for some bags, fusible fleece) for most of the projects in this book. Keep in mind that extra fabric may be needed to match plaids, stripes, and nap.

Exterior fashion fabrics: Quilting cotton, cotton canvas, lightweight corduroy, twill, linen, decorator-weight fabric, wool, flannel

Lining: Chambray, quilting cotton, cotton lawn, poplin

Interfacing and fusible fleece: Pellon SF101 Shape-Flex interfacing and your favorite fusible fleece

Getting Started

Before you start sewing, you'll need to gather some basic sewing tools and supplies and learn a few techniques. Practice makes perfect! A few basic techniques are all you need to know to make some great handbags, but there are specialty techniques demonstrated throughout the project pages. Read on!

Sewing Tools

To produce the best sewing results, it helps to have the right tools for the job. So as not to overwhelm you, I suggest that you get what you need for the project you are working on and build from there. Here is a list of basic tools you'll need for almost every project in this book.

Basic Sewing Tool Kit

You'll need the following must-have tools to make all the projects in this book:

- Sewing machine

- Hand and machine sewing needles

- Iron and ironing board

- Pattern paper

- Pins

- Scissors: One pair for cutting paper and one pair for cutting fabric

- Tailor's chalk or water-soluble marking pen

- Thread

Here's a bit of information about the various sewing tools.

- **GENERAL-PURPOSE POLYESTER THREAD**
  Choose a shade darker than the fabric because thread color is lighter than it appears on the spool. You might also pick up a spool of heavyweight (buttonhole twist) for hand sewing.

- **CUTTING TOOLS**

  Paper scissors are for cutting paper.

  Fabric shears are 8″–9″ long and are used to cut fabric. They are a bit heavy.

  Fabric scissors are smaller than shears, and you can use them to trim seam allowances.

  Snips are small scissors that you use to trim threads and clip into the seam allowance.

  Pinking shears cut a zigzag edge to prevent raveling threads.

  A **seam ripper** helps you pull out stitches and correct stitching mistakes. Everyone needs one!

  ### Tip

  Don't ever use your fabric scissors to cut paper! It can dull the blades.

- **MARKING TOOLS**

  Tailor's chalk

  Water-soluble fabric-marking pen

  ### Tip

  Be sure to test marking tools on scrap fabric before using them on your good fabric.

- **NEEDLES AND PINS IN A VARIETY OF SIZES AND A PINCUSHION**

  ### Tip

  I like the tomato pincushion with the little strawberry. The strawberry is filled with emery abrasives to sharpen and clean needles.

- **MEASURING TOOLS**

  Seam gauge to mark the width of the seam or hem

  Quilt rulers, in a variety of sizes, to draw marking lines, mark darts, and help with rotary cutting

  Ezy-Hem Gauge (a metal pressing ruler with markings on both sides)

  ### Tip

  Design rulers function like most office or school rulers; they measure distance. However, some have very specific markings for design tasks. For the projects in this book, I like a variety of quilting rulers. These rulers have markings at ⅛″ increments and deep right angles to assist with drawing a good corner square.

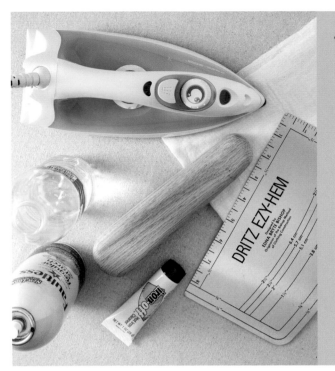

- **PRESSING TOOLS**

  Steam iron with adjustable heat settings

  Iron soleplate cleaning solution

  Ironing board, mat, or quilt board

  Pressing cloth to protect the iron and the fabric (An old cotton rag works!)

  Clapper for pressing steam into fabric to help flatten seams

  Pressing mate for accurate hemming and seam finishes

  Water bottle to refill the steam chamber

  Spray starch to add stiffness to fabric so it is easy to sew

Bag-Making Hardware and Tools

Magnetic snaps come in a range of colors and sizes. They are easy to insert.

Cap rivets are used for finishing and reinforcing leather and bag details.

D-rings are D-shaped metal rings used for fastening handles to bags.

Adjustable sliders are used to thread a strap and to adjust the length.

Swivel snap hooks are used with D-rings to clip straps to a bag.

Eyelets are small round pieces of metal used for finishing and reinforcing fabric holes.

Grommets are like eyelets, only larger.

Tip
You need an eyelet setter and hammer tools to insert eyelets and grommets in fabric.

Hand Sewing

Sometimes a bit of hand sewing is needed to finish up some of the projects.

Threading a Needle

1. Snip the end of the thread at a 45° angle.

2. Hold the needle at a tilt so you can see the eye (the hole at the top of the needle).

3. With the other hand, push a bit of thread through the eye.

4. Grab the thread and pull it through. *fig. A*

5. Loop the thread end(s) around your finger and tie a simple knot. *fig. B*

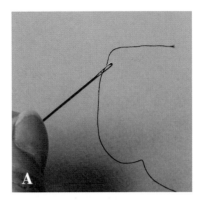

A

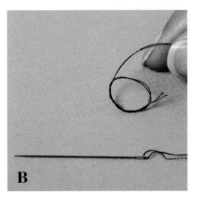

B

Tip

Cut the thread so it is equal in length to the distance between your fingertips and your elbow. This will help prevent the thread from knotting and fraying.

Sewing a Running Stitch

This is the hand-sewing stitch I use most often. You can use it to sew the opening of the lining closed in several of the projects.

Insert the needle through fabric and pull through. Continue stitching, making the length of the stitches equal to the length of the spaces between the stitches.

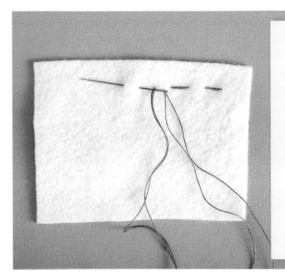

Tip

Consider this stitch like a dashed line. Instead of using a marker, you're using a needle and thread. Visualize the space of the stitch as well as the negative space in between. My goal is to make both the stitches and the spaces even and consistent.

Machine Sewing

First you need to get comfortable with your sewing machine and then practice a few things, like sewing a straight seam, turning a corner, and sewing around curves.

Getting to Know Your Sewing Machine

Every machine looks different, but most of them have the same parts. Your user's guide or manual will explain the parts of your sewing machine and the basic mechanics, so keep it handy!

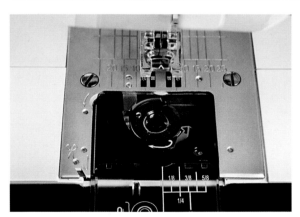

You do need to know about the bobbin before you can sew. The bobbin is a tiny spool that holds the thread for the stitches that form on the bottom of the fabric. Check your manual!

You'll probably notice thread path guides printed on your machine with a colored line or a series of dots. One set of markings is to show you how to thread the machine from the thread spool to the needle, and the other probably shows you how to fill a bobbin.

Again, the owner's manual will be very helpful until you know how to make a bobbin and how to thread your machine without even thinking about it.

General Guide for Threading a Sewing Machine

1. Raise the presser foot.

2. Place the spool of thread on the spindle and secure it with the end cap.

3. Pull the end of the thread from the spool along the top of the machine to the thread guides on the top of the machine.

4. Draw the thread between the tension discs and then down toward the needle.

5. Hold the thread taught and guide it back toward the take-up lever.

6. Guide the thread around the take-up lever. (Again, every machine is a bit different.)

7. Pull the thread through the remaining thread guide toward the needle.

8. Give the thread end a fresh cut at a 45° angle so that it goes through the needle easier.

9. Guide the thread through the slit in the presser foot.

General Guide for Threading a Bobbin

Some machines have a drop-in bobbin and others have a case which holds the bobbin. Regardless, the bobbin is almost always found under the throat plate near the presser foot. Check your manual for more about your bobbin.

1. Wind a bobbin on the top of the sewing machine, following the threading guides and your owner's manual.

2. Place the bobbin in the machine, making sure that the thread tail follows the threading guide on the machine or the instructions in the manual.

3. Pull the bobbin thread tail up through the bottom of the sewing machine. I use my left hand to hold the needle thread tail and turn the hand wheel toward me with my right hand to lower the needle into the machine to draw up the bobbin thread. In class, we call this "going fishing!"

4. Very carefully grab both threads (you may need to slide the bobbin plate or a pair of scissors under the presser foot to clear the threads) and pull them to the back left of the machine. You are ready to sew!

Operating the Sewing Machine

Now it's time to sew!

1. Make sure that both the top and bottom threads are pulled toward the back left side of your machine. The top thread should pass through the notch in the presser foot with the bottom thread (bobbin) just underneath. These threads work together to form the stitches. *fig. A*

2. Lower the presser foot. As you start to stitch, hold the thread ends with your left hand for just a few stitches. Once you take a few stitches, you can let go of the thread ends and allow the machine to feed your fabric through as you continue stitching. This frees up your hands to guide the fabric.

3. Notice that there are marked seam guidelines on your sewing machine to the right of the presser foot. The guidelines are usually ¼″, ½″, and even ⅝″ away from the needle so you can guide the edge of the fabric along the guidelines and the stitches will be the correct distance away from the fabric edge. Measure the distance from the stitched line to the edge of the fabric to be sure your seam is correct.

4. Position your hands so that they can comfortably guide or steer the fabric. When teaching someone to sew for the first time, I often have them sew for just a minute without using their hands so that they can see how the feed dogs work—kind of like a conveyer belt! If the fabric begins to slide, then use your hands to guide it back on track. Try it!

5. Lastly, you need to know about the reverse button. The reverse feature essentially ties a knot. You push the reverse button down for 2–3 stitches. Generally, this is done at the beginning and end of a seam to secure the stitches.

A

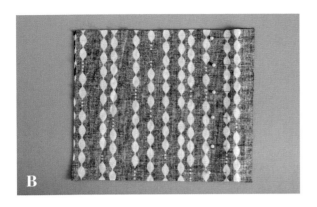

Sewing a Seam

Most seams are sewn with right sides of the fabrics facing together. This means that the pretty sides are pinned together. Here is a quick seam-stitching lesson.

1. Cut 2 squares 8″ × 8″ of scrap fabric.

2. Pin the pieces along one side with right sides together and the edges aligned. *fig. B*

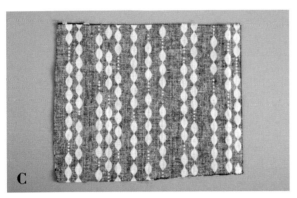

3. Stitch. Reverse stitch at the beginning and end of the seam so the stitches don't pull out. Snip the threads. *fig. C*

4. Open the seam, and press the seam allowances open. *fig. D*

5. Marvel at your accomplishment! *fig. E*

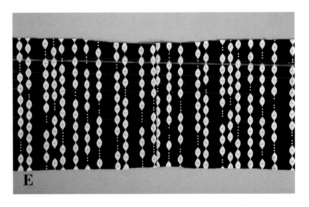

Turning a Corner

To add design lines and shape to your project, you often need to stitch around a corner. It sounds much trickier than it is! Take your time, and this will soon be second nature.

1. Mark a dot ½˝ away from each corner.

2. Sew a straight seam along one side of the fabric and stop, with the needle down, when you get to the dot. Make sure that the needle is in the fabric. If it's not, use the handwheel to reposition the needle. *fig. A*

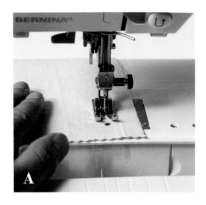

3. Lift the presser foot, rotate the fabric 90° (a right angle), lower the presser foot, and continue sewing. *fig. B*

Sewing a Curved Seam

The most important thing to remember when sewing a curved seam is to take your time and keep an even and consistent seam allowance. This may take some practice, but that's why we are here, right? You've got this!

1. Mark the curve with tailor's chalk or a water-soluble fabric pen. *fig. C*

2. Pin the seam with a lot of pins.

3. Shorten the stitch length to improve accuracy.

4. Stitch from pin to pin, removing each pin so that you don't stitch over it. Make sure that the machine needle is positioned correctly to stay along the path. *fig. D*

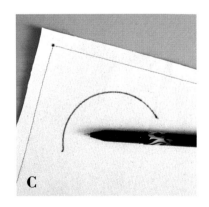

5. Notch around the curved edge or trim with pinking shears, cutting close to the seam but not through it.

Tip

To notch is to cut little triangles out of the seam allowance. This helps shape the curved seam. Alternately, you can use pinking shears.

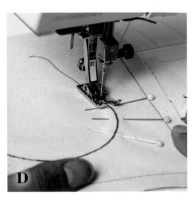

Applying Fusibles

Every type of fusible product has a preferred application method, and instructions do come with the purchase. Be sure to read the manufacturer's instructions prior to fusing. Generally, you need to use a damp pressing cloth and the steam setting on your iron to adhere the interfacing or fleece properly. You might want to trim the interfacing and fleece ½˝ smaller than the fabric piece all around to reduce bulk in the seams. If the fabric is lightweight, this might not be necessary. If you want to add a layer of fusible fleece for a bit more support, follow the same instructions as for interfacing and fuse the fleece directly over the interfacing. Always pretest on a piece of scrap fabric.

1. Trim the interfacing ⅜˝–½˝ smaller than the pattern, if desired, to reduce bulk.

2. Press the fabric so it is flat and smooth.

3. If you have a high-heat steam setting on your iron, steam the fabric to preshrink it slightly. This will prevent the interfacing from bubbling.

4. Run your hand over the interfacing to determine the side with the adhesive (or glue). It will feel rougher than the other side. Position the interfacing on the wrong side of the fabric with the adhesive side down. If you are using multiple pieces, overlap them ⅛˝.

5. Set your iron to the steam setting with water in the receptacle.

6. Cover the fabric and interfacing with a damp pressing cloth to protect the iron and the fabric.

7. Press, holding the iron in place for a few seconds. Lift the iron and repeat to press the remainder of the interfacing (or fleece) to the fabric. Use an up-and-down (*not* back-and-forth) motion.

Pressing

Pressing is an up-and-down motion, not a side-to-side motion, and it is such an important part of the sewing process. It infinitely improves the look of your work, making seams appear straight and crisp. You really should stitch and then press. And stitch and then press again!

A few tips:

- Press seam allowances open and then flat.

- *Never* touch the metal soleplate. It might be hot!

- Don't leave the iron on the fabric for long. A few seconds should do it.

- When you are finished pressing, empty the water chamber.

- Keep the soleplate clean.

Making Embellishments

What Is a Focal Point?

As we discussed in Proportion, Scale, and Harmony (page 12), separate elements come together to form a whole. Essentially, a **focal point** is the design element to which you want to draw attention. The eye naturally follows lines; by creating a strong visual statement, you give the eye a place to settle.

A focal point emphasizes one element over all the rest. It says, "Hello!" Here's a design hint: You need one focal point. Notice that I used the word *one*. This is where the "less is more" philosophy comes into play. Simple is best, and this means asking yourself, "I know I can add this to my design, but should I?" Some of the trims and embellishments used in this book are really easy and fun to make!

Pom-Poms

Pom-poms aren't just for backpacks anymore! As far as fashion goes, fancy and elegant accessories have always been typecast for evening, with no-nonsense accessories restricted to daytime. Well, listen up—those rules are meant to be broken! Accessories that blur the boundaries between daytime and evening—even the humble wrapped-yarn pompom—break all those boring rules. Accessories are meant to be noticed anywhere and anytime!

Materials

COLORFUL YARN

POM-POM–MAKING TOOL
(I use The Loome.)

SCISSORS

CRAFT THREAD

There are a lot of different pom-pom–making tools. I like to use The Loome.

Making a Pom-Pom

1. Begin by reviewing the instructions on the tool packaging.

2. Wrap yarn approximately 100 times around the tool. Don't wrap the yarn too tightly or it will be difficult to remove. *fig. A*

Tip

Sometimes I put my thumb between the tool and the wrapped yarn to keep it loose.

3. Once you have enough yarn wrapped around the tool, cut the yarn. Cut a length of string or craft thread about 18″ long. Wrap the string around the center of the bundle of wrapped yarn and tie a knot. Pull the wrap of yarn off the maker and wrap the length of string twice around the center again; tie it tightly. Doesn't it look like a bow? *fig. B*

4. Cut the loops open, but don't cut the string. You will need it to attach your pom-pom! *fig. C*

5. Now give the pom-pom a haircut to shape it and even out the ends. So fun, right? *fig. D*

6. Use the strings to secure the pom-pom to whatever needs a focal point or just a colorful accessory.

A

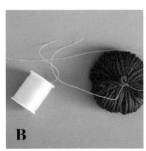

B

C

D

Cotton Jersey Bag Charms

These bag charms are fun to make and to share.

Materials

COTTON JERSEY FABRIC: 10″ × 3″

ASSORTED BEADS

WIDE-EYE NEEDLE

SCISSORS

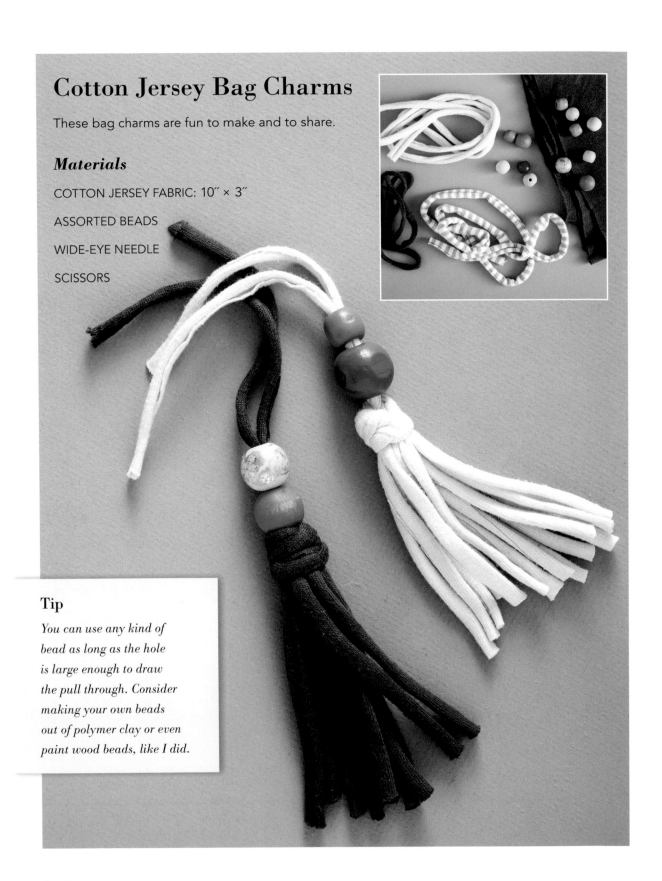

Tip

You can use any kind of bead as long as the hole is large enough to draw the pull through. Consider making your own beads out of polymer clay or even paint wood beads, like I did.

Making the Bag Charm

1. Cut the jersey fabric on the straight grain into 6 pieces, each 10″ × ½″.

2. Gently pull on the 6 strands of jersey to stretch and curl them. *fig. A*

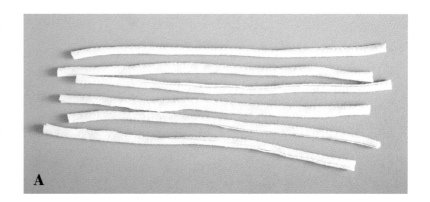

A

3. Bend 5 of the strands together on a table in a U shape, with the remaining strand across them, as shown. *fig. B*

4. Fold the 10 strand ends into the curve of the U shape, as shown. *fig. C*

5. Pull to the strands to tighten the knot. *fig. D*

6. Trim the ends so the strands are even.

7. Embellish the tassel with beads. *fig. E*

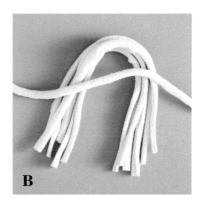

B

C

D

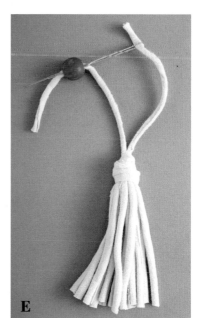

E

Tip

If you don't have a needle large enough for your tassel strand, make one! Unfold both ends of a paper clip and use a pair of pliers to pinch the last fold small enough to fit through the bead.

Leather Tassels

For long-lasting tassels and bag charms, make them out of scraps of leather.

Materials

LEATHER SCRAPS

ADHESIVE, such as E6000
(*Caution:* This can be messy.)

MAT to protect table

ROTARY CUTTER

TRANSPARENT RULER

PENCIL

METAL SWIVEL HOOK

METALLIC THREAD *or* EMBROIDERY FLOSS

Tip

It is easier to cut strips of leather with a rotary cutter than with scissors. You'll also need a cutting mat to protect the table and a ruler to help measure out even strips. You might need adult help to use the rotary cutter—the blade is very sharp.

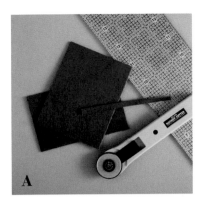

A

1. Cut out 3 pieces of leather in the following sizes: 4″ × 2½″, 4″ × 3″, and 4″ × ¼″. *fig. A*

2. Use a pencil and ruler to draw a straight line across the top of each piece, ½″ from the top edge. *fig. B*

3. Cut ⅛″-wide strips across all of the pieces, from the bottom edge up to, but not through, the line you drew, as shown. *fig. C*

4. Center the medium-size piece on top of the largest piece. Between those 2 pieces, insert the narrowest piece sticking straight up and glue them together along the top edges. *fig. D*

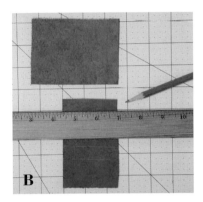

B

5. Thread the end of the narrowest strip through the swivel hook and glue it down. *figs. E & F*

6. Squeeze a bead of glue across the line that you drew in Step 2. Begin to fold and tightly roll the leather inward from right to left.

7. Pinch the roll for a minute or two to allow the adhesive to set.

8. Your tassel is complete! I chose to take it a step further and add a little more glam. Cut a 30″ length of metallic thread or embroidery floss (or both!) to wrap around the tassel.

C

9. Tie a slipknot with the metallic thread. Fit it over the tassel, slip it into position, and tighten the knot. Begin to wrap the thread until you achieve the desired width. Smear a bead of glue onto the floss and press. Set aside to dry.

Tip

Imagine the fun effect of multiple colors and layers of wrapped floss and fringed leather.

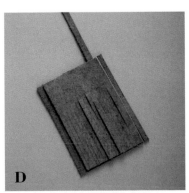

D

E

F

Labels

Adding a label to your design is super easy and really fun. You can try different methods and materials to imbue your bag with an extra dash of style. Let your imagination be your guide.

Supplies

You can use almost anything to make labels, such as twill tape, scraps of leather, kraft-tex, and lightweight vinyl. It also helps to have pinking shears, a hole punch, a leather stamping kit, a hammer or mallet, washi tape, a leather punch tool, a hand-sewing needle, scissors, and/or embroidery floss handy.

Whichever way you want to make labels is really up to you! Here are a few examples—but remember, like all design work, it's a good idea to practice on a sheet of scrap paper first and then trace your design onto your final label material. Squares, rectangles, circles, elongated ovals—think of this exercise as your way to brand your design. Embellish it with your initials, name, or a fun design! Then simply sew or glue the label to the inside lining or even on the outside of your bag. Have fun with it!

Make a Leather Label

1. Cut out the label material to your desired shape and size. Measure to make sure there is space to stamp or draw a design. *fig. A*

2. Dampen the leather before stamping for a better impression. Place the stamp where you want it on the leather and give it a firm tap. Watch your fingers! *fig. B*

3. If you want to sew your label onto a project, you will need holes. Determine how many holes and where you would like them placed. It helps to mark them with a pencil. Place and align the leather piece in the punch. Give the handle a good squeeze to punch it through the leather. *fig. C*

Tip

You can place a piece of washi tape along the label to help line up your letters!

A

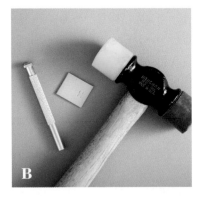

B

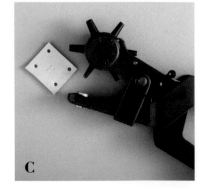

C

Projects

Now that you have a good understanding of the basic concepts, it's time to apply that design knowledge. You can make a bag for every day of the week, every special occasion, or just because— they are just so fun to make and to have!

When you make all the different bags in this book, you'll learn so much about sewing, including the basics such as pattern marking, using interfacing, sewing curves and corners, making double-fold straps, and a whole lot more!

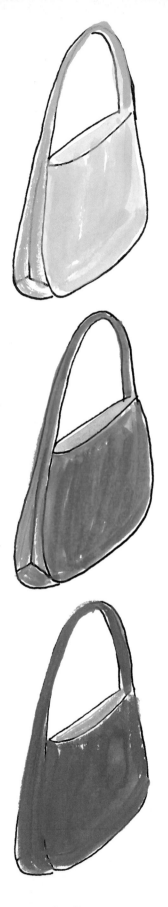

Easy Shoulder-Strap Bags

Morganne Simple Little Purse

This sweet little purse is a great introduction to the art of
bag making! It's quick to sew and makes a perfect gift!

FINISHED SIZE:
9¾″ wide × 7½″ tall

Supplies

Cotton yardage is based on 44"-wide fabric.

FABRIC A: ⅝ yard of medium-weight to heavyweight cotton for bag exterior

FABRIC B: 1 fat quarter (or 11" × 22" piece) of contrasting lightweight cotton for lining

INTERFACING: ⅜ yard

BASIC SEWING TOOL KIT (page 24)

PATTERN 1 (front and back; pullout page P1)

Cutting

FABRIC A (EXTERIOR AND STRAP)

- Cut 1 from pattern 1.
- Cut 1 strap 3" × 44".

FABRIC B (LINING)

- Cut 1 from pattern 1.

INTERFACING

- Cut 1 from pattern 1.
- Cut 2 strips 2½" × 20" and 1 strip 2½" × 3¼" for the strap.

Prepare

1. Trace pattern 1 and all the markings onto pattern paper. Cut out the paper pattern.

2. Mark the cutting dimensions for the strap on a single layer of the exterior fabric with chalk or a fabric-marking pen. Cut out the strap.

3. Pin the pattern onto a double layer of the exterior fabric, with the pattern fold line positioned along the fabric fold.

4. Transfer the pattern markings to the fabric (page 19).

5. Cut out the fabric around the outside pattern lines.

6. Repeat Steps 3–5 to cut out pattern 1 from the lining fabric.

7. Fuse the interfacing to the wrong side of the exterior bag fabric and to the strap, placing the strap pieces ½" from each end and overlapped ⅛". Refer to Applying Fusibles (page 33) for more information. *figs. A & B*

A

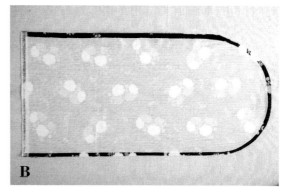

B

Make the Bag

All seams are sewn with a ½˝ seam allowance unless otherwise noted.

1. Pin the bag exterior to the lining with right sides together.

2. Sew around all the sides, leaving an opening between the 2 marked dots on the short straight side; reverse stitch at each dot. Trim the thread ends and diagonally cut away the corners. Use your pinking shears to trim around the curved edge. Be careful to cut close to the seam but not through it! *figs. C & D*

3. Turn your bag right side out through the opening. Use your finger to carefully poke out the corners so they form a nice right angle. (Sometimes I use a straight pin to carefully "pick" the corners out.) Press. *fig. E*

4. Press the seam allowances at the 4˝ opening to the inside and then edgestitch along that entire side, sewing the opening closed as you stitch. Set the bag aside. *fig. F*

5. Make a double-fold strap (page 47). Measure and mark a removable dot 4˝ from each end.

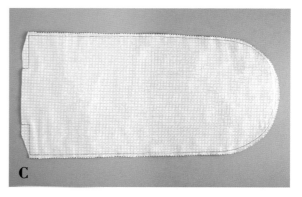

C

D

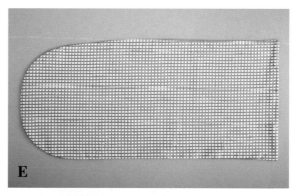

E

F

Put It All Together

1. To finish, position the bag on your work surface with the outside fabric facing down. Fold the bottom edge of the bag up 7¼″ so it aligns with the marked dots on each side edge.

2. Pin each end of the strap at the matching dots along the left and right sides. Slant the ends of the strap slightly so the flap lays correctly when you are wearing the bag.

3. Use a ¼″ seam allowance to sew through all of the layers on the left and right sides of the bag. This closes the sides of the bag and creates a neat top-stitch detail along the sides. *fig. G*

4. Press one more time. You are done!

G

Tip

Make the bag again, but this time try changing a detail. If you omit the straps, use sumptuous fabric, and add a magnetic clasp, the same bag suddenly turns into a fancy evening clutch. A chain handle is another exciting option!

Making Straps

Making straps for your handbag is super easy and fun. You can try different methods and materials. For the bags in this book, I've kept the straps simple, but simple doesn't mean your options are limited in any way. When you think about all the different colors, textures, widths, and lengths, you'll know you have options!

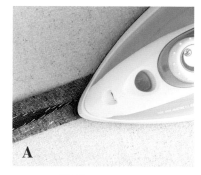

Tip

You can always purchase webbing or strapping from the store to create super-cool straps. However, it is easy to sew fabric straps, and I'll show you two straightforward sewing methods that yield fantastic and durable results.

Double-Fold Strap

Most of the straps in this book are double folded. I generally make a double-fold strap when the finished width of the strap is too narrow to sew and turn a single fold or when the fabric is bulky.

1. Cut the fabric to the length and width indicated in the instructions. Fuse interfacing to the wrong side of the strap if the pattern calls for it or if you want to make the strap a bit stiffer. Press the strap in half lengthwise with wrong sides together.

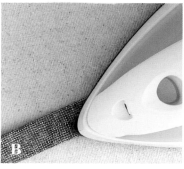

2. Open the strap and fold both raw edges so they meet in the middle. Press. *fig. A*

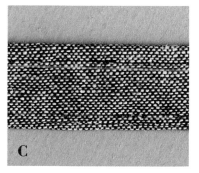

3. Fold the strap in half again along the center crease and press. *fig. B*

4. Pin the strap closed and topstitch ⅛″ from each long edge. Press the strap again. *fig. C*

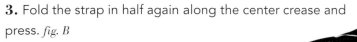

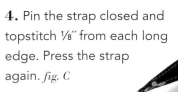

Morganne Simple Little Purse   47

Single-Fold Strap

A single-fold strap is usually a bit wider than a double-fold strap and is easy to turn right side out. Refer to the bag instructions for the desired width and length. You usually don't use interfacing for a single-fold strap because the added bulk makes it harder to turn the strap right side out.

1. Cut the fabric to the length and width indicated in the instructions. Fold the strap in half lengthwise with right sides together. Stitch the open long edge closed with a ½″ seam allowance. *fig. D*

2. Press the seam and trim the seam allowance.

3. Turn the strap right side out and topstitch ⅛″ from each long edge. Press. *fig. E*

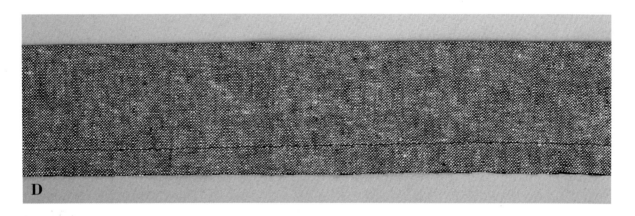

D

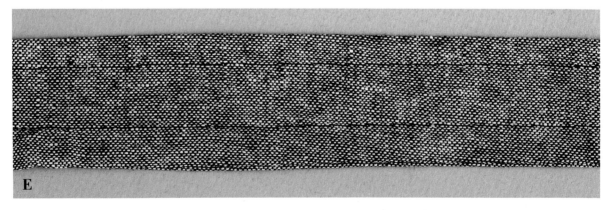

E

Wesley Shoulder Bag

This shoulder bag is endlessly versatile and lends itself to all kinds of fabric options.

FINISHED SIZE:
12˝ wide × 8˝ tall × 4˝ deep

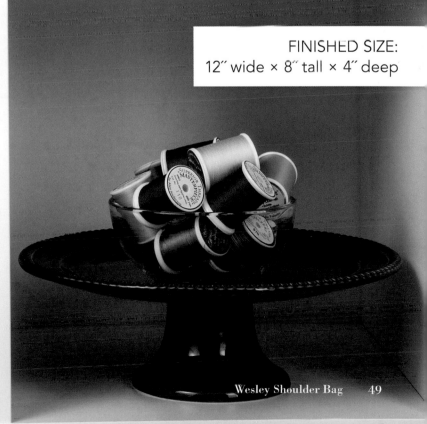

Supplies

Cotton yardage is based on 44″-wide fabric.

FABRIC A: ⅝ yard of medium-weight to heavyweight cotton for bag exterior

FABRIC B: ½ yard of contrasting lightweight cotton for lining

INTERFACING: ¾ yard

BASIC SEWING TOOL KIT (page 24)

PATTERN 7 (front and back; pullout page P2)

Cutting

FABRIC A

- Cut 2 from pattern 7.
- Cut 2 straps, each 3″ × 20″.

FABRIC B

- Cut 2 from pattern 7.

INTERFACING

- Cut 2 from pattern 7.
- Cut 2 strips 2½″ × 19″.

Tip

This bag is a good candidate for adding fusible fleece if you want the sides a bit sturdier. It's up to you!

Prepare

1. Trace pattern 7 and all the markings onto pattern paper. Cut out the paper pattern.

2. Fold fabric A in half, right sides together, and mark the cutting dimensions for the strap with chalk or a fabric-marking pen. Cut 2 straps.

3. Pin the pattern onto the double layer of fabric A, with the pattern fold line positioned along the fabric fold. Allow room to cut this pattern 2 times on the fabric fold. You might want to fold each selvage into toward the center of the fabric so you have 2 fabric folds.

4. Transfer the pattern markings to the fabric (page 19). Cut out the fabric.

5. Repeat Steps 3 and 4 to cut pattern 7 from fabric B and interfacing.

6. Trim the interfacing for the bag pieces ⅜″–½″ all around so they are bit smaller than the exterior fabric pieces. Fuse the interfacing to the wrong side of the exterior front and back bag pieces and to both strap pieces (see Applying Fusibles, page 33).

Make the Bag

All seams are sewn with a ½″ seam allowance unless otherwise noted.

1. Pin and sew the sides and bottom of the fabric A bag pieces with right sides together. Refer to Sewing a Curved Seam (page 32). *fig. A*

2. Pin and sew the sides and bottom of the fabric B pieces with right sides together, leaving the bottom edge unstitched between the marked dots. Backstitch at the marked dots along the bottom edge. This opening makes it possible to turn the bag right side out later. *fig. B*

3. Trim the thread ends and notch around the curved edge. Be careful to cut close to the seam but not through it!

4. Make 2 single-fold straps (page 48).

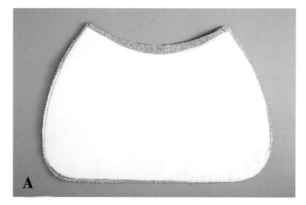

A

B

Put It All Together

1. To assemble the bag, pin each end of one strap to the exterior front, ¼″ from the side seam, with the strap's raw edges at an angle to the bag's top edge. Repeat for the bag back strap. Make sure the straps are not twisted. *fig. C*

C

2. Hand or machine baste the strap ends in place and trim off the excess strap. Turn the bag so the wrong side is facing out. Slide the lining inside the bag so the right sides are together and the seams are aligned.

3. Pin the lining and bag together along the top edge, with the straps tucked between them. Stitch the entire top edge, catching the straps as you stitch. *fig. D*

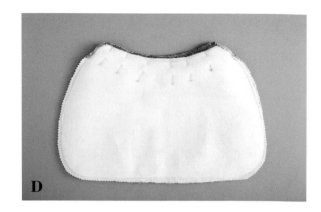

D

4. Turn your bag right side out through the opening in the lining. Run your hand inside the curve to help shape and mold the seam so it is smooth.

5. Understitch the seam on the lining side. *fig. E*

E

Understitching Tip

Understitching helps hold the lining inside the bag so it doesn't roll to the right side and look funny. To understitch, extend the bag and the lining away from each other and press the seam. Stitch through both the right side of the lining fabric as well as the seam allowance, ⅛" away from the exterior piece.

6. Press the seam allowances in the opening of the lining toward the inside of the bag and hand sew the lining closed. Tuck the lining into the bag and press the top edge.

7. To create a bottom edge to the bag, refer to the markings on the pattern and see Making a Flat Bottom with Boxed Corners, Method 3 (page 69).

Making an Inverted Box Pleat

Pattern shaping helps you transform a flat piece of fabric into a dimensional object with endless possibilities. From a construction point of view, there are several beautiful and clever details that can be created by folding fabric. Pleats and tucks are two shaping techniques that add dimension, shape, and depth to a design. There are many different types of pleats: box pleats, knife pleats, kick pleats, and Fortuny pleats to name just a few. It's easy to make an inverted box pleat, which happens to be a traditional box pleat that is flipped over. The Savannah Cross-Body Bag (page 55) has an inverted pleat that is stitched to create a narrow opening and fuller curved bottom. This geometric detail, as interpreted through the prism of design, adds overall balance to a very simple bag.

1. Mark the pleat fold lines (3 short straight lines) on the fabric.

Inverted box pleat

2. Fold the fabric with right sides together along the inside marked pleat line; pin. Stitch along the outside marked lines. Backstitch at the beginning and end of the stitching.

3. Flip the fabric so the wrong side is facing up. Open the stitched pleat and then flatten it as shown. Press and pin the pleat into place.

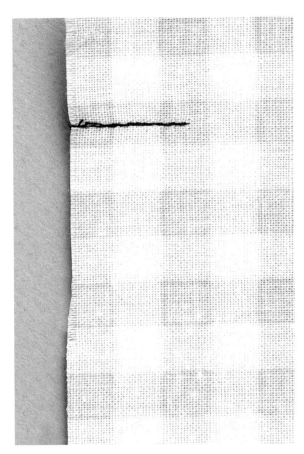 

Tip

Tucks are another easy way to create shape. A tuck is essentially a single-fold stitched pleat that is used to shape or control fullness. The tuck can be stitched to the right or wrong side of a bag.

Savannah Cross-Body Bag

This modern cross-body bag is the perfect size for holding all your essentials. It features a center pleat for a little extra flair.

FINISHED SIZE:
9¾˝ wide × 8½˝ tall

Supplies

Cotton yardage is based on 44″-wide fabric.

FABRIC A: ⅜ yard of medium-weight to heavyweight cotton for bag exterior

FABRIC B: ⅜ yard of contrasting lightweight cotton for lining

INTERFACING: ½ yard

2 D-RINGS (**½″** DIAMETER)

BASIC SEWING TOOL KIT (page 24)

PATTERN PIECES 2 AND 3 (front and back, and facing; pullout page P1)

Cutting

FABRIC A

- Cut 2 each from patterns 2 and 3.

- Cut 1 strap 3″ × 44″ and 1 tab 3″ × 6″.

FABRIC B

- Cut 2 from pattern 2.

INTERFACING

- Cut 2 from pattern 3.

- Cut 3 strips 2″ × 20″ for the strap and tab.

Prepare

1. Trace both patterns 2 and 3, and all the markings, onto pattern paper. Cut out the paper patterns.

2. Mark the cutting dimensions for the strap and tabs on a double layer of the exterior fabric and on a double layer of interfacing with chalk or a fabric-marking pen. Cut out the straps and tabs.

3. Fold fabric A in half, right sides together, and pin patterns 2 and 3 to the double layer of fabric.

4. Transfer the pattern markings to the fabric (page 19). Cut out the fabric.

5. Repeat Steps 3 and 4 to cut pattern 2 from fabric B.

6. Fold a double layer of interfacing and pin pattern 3 to the double layer. Cut out the interfacing. Trim the interfacing so it is ⅜″–½″ smaller all around than the fabric pieces. Trim the 2″ × 20″ pieces to fit the strap and tab, placing them ½″ from each end and overlapping ⅛″.

7. Fuse the interfacing to the wrong side of the facing, strap, and tab pieces (see Applying Fusibles, page 33).

Make the Bag

All seams are sewn with a ½″ seam allowance unless otherwise noted.

1. Refer to Making an Inverted Box Pleat (page 53) and the pattern markings to make an inverted pleat in the bag front and bag back of both the fabric A pieces and the fabric B pieces.

2. Pin and sew the sides and bottom of the fabric A pieces with right sides together, referring to Sewing a Curved Seam (page 32). Repeat with the fabric B pieces. *fig. A*

3. Trim the thread ends and notch around the curved edges. Be careful to cut close to the seam but not through it!

4. Make a double-fold strap with both strap/tab pieces (page 47). From the 6″ finished tab, cut 2 sections 3″ long for the D-ring tabs. Thread a tab through 1 D-ring and stitch the ends together to secure the tab and D-ring together. Repeat with the remaining tab and D-ring. Set these aside until later. *fig. B*

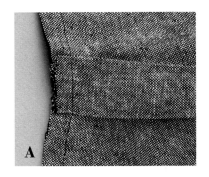

A

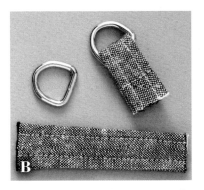

B

Make the Facing

1. With right sides together, sew the short edges of the facing pieces together. *fig. C*

2. Fold one long edge ½″ to the wrong side and press. *fig. D*

3. Stitch the folded edge in place and press.

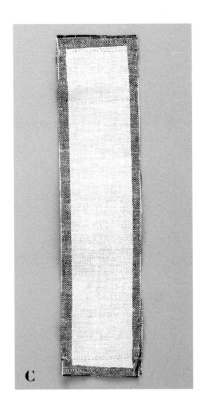

C

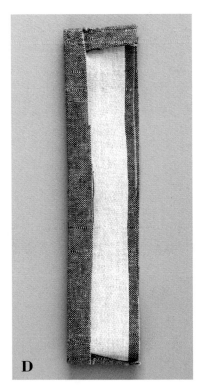

D

Put It All Together

1. To assemble the bag, turn the exterior bag right side out and slide the lining inside the bag so that the *wrong* sides are together. Align the side seams, pleats, and top openings. Pin the top edges together.

2. Baste the exterior bag and lining together around the top edge.

3. Pin the ends of the tabs to the right side of the bag at the side seams so all edges align and the D-rings fall toward the right side of the bag. Baste the tab ends to the top of the bag.

4. Pin the facing to the top of the bag with right sides together and the facing seams aligned with the side seams. Stitch this seam, catching the tab ends in the stitching. *fig. E*

5. Press the seam. Understitch (page 52) ⅛″ away from the seamline through both the right side of the facing and the seam allowance.

6. Press the facing to the inside of the bag and extend the tabs out of the bag.

7. Thread the strap ends through each of the D-rings on the bag. Tuck the raw edges under and stitch the fold to the strap to secure the strap to the D-rings.

E

Sarah Shoulder Bag

Step out in style with a sophisticated shoulder bag with a gusset and fold-over flap.

Add a length of beautiful decorative trim to give it your own special signature.

FINISHED SIZE:
10˝ wide × 5½˝ tall × 1½˝ deep

Supplies

Cotton yardage is based on 44″-wide fabric.

FABRIC A: ⅜ yard of medium-weight to heavyweight cotton for bag exterior

FABRIC B: ⅜ yard of contrasting lightweight cotton for lining

INTERFACING: ⅝ yard

FUSIBLE FLEECE: ½ yard

2 D-RINGS (1″ WIDE)

DECORATIVE TRIM (1⅜″ WIDE): 8″ piece

BASIC SEWING TOOL KIT (page 24)

PATTERN PIECES 4, 5, AND 6 (front and back, flap, and gusset; pullout pages P1 and P2)

Cutting

FABRIC A

- Cut 2 from pattern 4.
- Cut 2 from pattern 5.
- Cut 1 from pattern 6.
- Cut 1 strap/tabs 3″ × 44″.

FABRIC B

- Cut 2 from pattern 4.
- Cut 1 from pattern 6.

INTERFACING AND FUSIBLE FLEECE

- Cut 2 from pattern 4.
- Cut 1 from pattern 5.
- Cut 1 from pattern 6.

INTERFACING

- Cut 2 strips 2″ × 20″ and 1 strip 2″ × 3¼″ for the strap and tabs.

Prepare

1. Trace patterns 4–6 and all the markings onto pattern paper. Cut out the paper patterns.

2. Mark the cutting dimensions for the strap and tabs on a single layer of the exterior fabric with chalk or a fabric-marking pen. Cut out the strap/tabs. Repeat to cut the strap/tabs from interfacing.

3. Fold the exterior fabric in half, right sides together. Pin patterns 4–6 onto the double layer of fabric, with the pattern 6 fold line positioned along the fabric fold.

4. Transfer the pattern markings to the fabric (page 19). Cut out the pieces.

5. Repeat Steps 3 and 4 to cut 2 of pattern 4 and 1 of pattern 6 (placed so pattern fold line is along fabric fold) from fabric B, fusible fleece, and interfacing. Trim the fusible fleece and interfacing so it is ⅜″–½″ smaller all around than the fabric pieces.

6. From a single layer of interfacing and fusible fleece, cut 1 of pattern 5.

7. Position the 2″ × 20″ interfacing pieces to fit the strap and tab, placing them ½″ from each end and overlapping ⅜″. Fuse the interfacing and then the fusible fleece to the wrong side of the exterior fabric pieces, 2 bag fronts and backs, 1 flap, and 1 gusset (see Applying Fusibles, page 33).

> ### Tip
>
> *I draw stitching lines on the fabric pieces to help align the gusset and front and back bag pieces. By matching these lines, your pieces should line up perfectly!*

Make the Bag

All seams are sewn with a ½″ seam allowance unless otherwise noted.

1. Pin the fabric A front to the gusset with right sides together. Match the markings and use a lot of pins along the curved edges to make it easier to ease the 2 pieces together. *fig. A*

2. Stitch the front to the gusset, stitching slowly around the curved sections and smoothing the fabric as you sew. Clip and trim the seam allowances. Press the seams. *fig. B*

3. Repeat to sew the fabric A back to the other side of the gusset.

A

> ### Tip
>
> *I find that if I stitch with the body side of the bag up and the gusset side down, I have more control over the shape.*

4. Repeat Steps 1–3 with the fabric B pieces.

5. Make a single-fold strap (page 48).

6. From the finished strap, cut 2 pieces 3″ long for the tabs. Insert each of these pieces through the D-rings and stitch the ends together to form tabs. Set the strap and tabs aside.

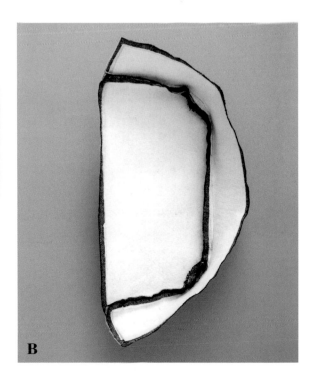

B

Make the Flap

1. Pin the decorative trim down the center of the flap, along the markings. Topstitch the trim to the front of the flap. *fig. C*

2. With right sides together, pin the 2 flap pieces together and stitch around all except the narrower edge. See Sewing a Curved Seam (page 32).

3. Trim the flap seam allowances with pinking shears and press the seam. *fig. D*

4. Turn the flap right side out and press.

5. Topstitch ¼″ away from the finished edges of the flap. Stitch slowly and carefully because these stitches will be visible. This is your time to shine!

C

D

Put It All Together

1. Turn the bag exterior right side out and pin a tab to each side, centered on the gusset and matching the raw edges. Baste the tab ends in place.

2. With the lining wrong side out, insert the exterior bag inside the lining with right sides together. Pin the top edges together, matching the gusset seams, with the tabs caught between them. *fig. A*

3. Stitch the top edges of the front and gusset together—do *not* stitch the top edge of the bag back. You need to leave this open so you can turn the bag right side out.

4. Understitch the seam (page 52).

5. Snip the thread ends and notch around the curved edge. Be careful to cut close to the seam but not through it! Refer to Sewing a Curved Seam (page 32).

6. Turn the bag right side out. Extend the tabs and D-rings up and outside the bag. Press the top edge of the back lining ½˝ to the wrong side.

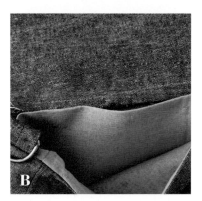

7. Pin the flap to the upper edge of the bag exterior with right sides together. Stitch without catching the lining, and trim the seam allowance.

8. Flip the flap up and encase the seam under the folded edge of the lining. Pin the lining in place to hide the seam allowance. *fig. B*

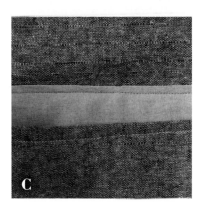

9. Stitch around the top edge of the bag through all layers. *fig. C*

10. Thread a strap end through each of the D-rings on the bag. Tuck the raw edges of the strap to the wrong side and stitch them to secure the strap.

Tote Bags

Susan Tote

There is a reason tote bags are classic. They are polished, practical, and provide space for everything you need to carry. Everyone should have a few, and they are so easy to make you can have one for every day of the week!

FINISHED SIZE:
16″ wide × 15″ tall

Supplies

Cotton yardage is based on 44˝-wide fabric.

FABRIC A: ⅝ yard of medium-weight to heavyweight cotton for tote exterior

COTTON WEBBING (1˝ WIDE): 1¾ yards

BASIC SEWING TOOL KIT (page 24)

Cutting

FABRIC A

- Cut 2 squares 17½˝ × 17½˝ for the bag front and back.

WEBBING

- Cut 2 straps 28˝ long.

Make the Tote

All seams are sewn with a ½˝ seam allowance unless otherwise noted.

1. Press the top edge of the bag front ½˝ toward the wrong side and then press again 1¼˝ toward the wrong side. Repeat for the bag back. *fig. A*

2. Position a webbing strap on the bag front by sliding the ends of the strap under the top folded edge, 4˝ from each side. Make sure the straps are not twisted. Pin in place. Repeat for the bag back. *fig. B*

3. Machine stitch ¼˝ from the bottom folded edge along the top of each bag piece, catching the straps in the stitching.

4. Flip the straps upward, press, and pin them in place.

5. Stitch the straps to the top edges of the front and back bag pieces. *fig. C*

Tip

You can always substitute fabric straps for webbing straps and vice versa! Just refer to Making Straps (page 47) and make sure you have enough fabric to cut the straps.

A

B

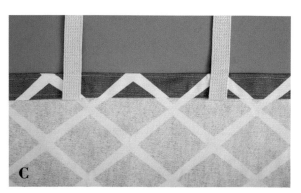

C

Put It All Together

1. Pin the bag front and back together so the *wrong* sides are facing. This is so you can stitch a French seam, which makes a nice clean finish inside the bag.

2. Stitch the sides and bottom edges with a ¼″ seam allowance. *fig. D*

3. Snip the thread ends. Turn the bag wrong side out and press.

4. Pin the seam to enclose the first seam. Stitch ½″ from the edge around all 3 sides of the bag. *fig. E*

5. Turn the tote bag right side out and enjoy! Wasn't that easy?

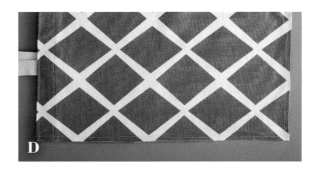

Note

Essentially, a French seam encases the raw edges to add strength to the seam and make it look as pretty on the inside as it does on the outside!

Making a Flat Bottom with Boxed Corners

So far, most of the bags we have made don't have a flat bottom. We learned that through adding pleats, darts, or a gusset, we can create shape. Another way to create shape or volume is by boxing the bottom of a bag. This creates a flat bottom with only a few extra sewing steps. It's easy and gives the bag a different look. There are three ways to box the bottom of a bag.

Making a Boxed Bottom

METHOD 1

1. If the patterns don't indicate a cutout at the sides seams and you want to make a boxed bottom, use a transparent ruler and tailor's chalk or a water-soluble pen to mark a 1½˝ square on the bottom corners of the front and back pieces. *fig. A*

2. Align and pin the bag front and bag back with right sides together. Stitch the sides and bottom edges. Snip the thread ends and press.

3. Open the corner cutouts and pinch them so that the side and bottom seams meet. Carefully pin the openings closed and stitch both corners, as shown. *fig. B*

4. Press and turn the bag right side out. Shape the corners to form the flat bottom. *fig. C*

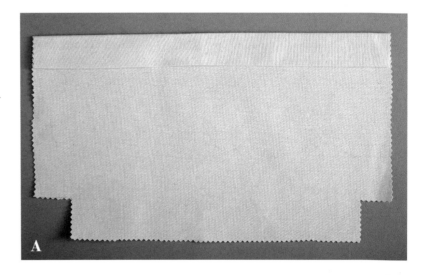

A

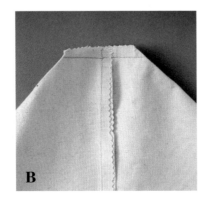

B

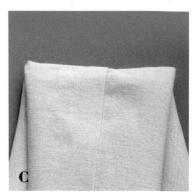

C

METHOD 2

Here is a way to make a boxed bottom if there isn't a bottom seam.

1. Fold the fabric in half with right sides together, matching the top and side edges. Stitch the bag side seams. Lightly press the bottom fold.

2. Flatten a side seam, matching the seam to the bottom fold.

3. Measure and mark a stitching line 2″–3″ from the pointed edge of the bag. Pin. Repeat for the other side. Stitch across the line on both sides of the bag. *fig. D*

4. Don't trim the triangle away—that bit of extra fabric tucks into the bottom of the bag to add strength and stability.

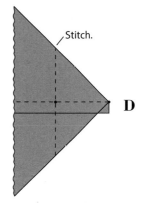

METHOD 3

There is one last way to make a box corner. This method adds a bit of a decorative effect.

1. Stitch the bag according to the pattern instructions.

2. Fold up the bottom marking to the side marking and pin the markings together (about 1½″ up the side seam).

3. Hand sew the markings together, and hide the knot by bringing your needle and thread to the inside of the bag to form the finishing knot. *figs. E & F*

Tip

You can hand sew this with coordinating thread to hide your stitching, but imagine how fabulous it would look with a decorative stitch and contrasting thread!

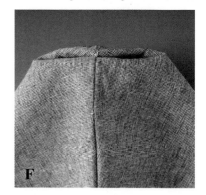

Heidi Side-Panel Tote

This medium-sized tote was designed to be the ultimate everyday bag. It features a side-panel gusset, webbing straps, a pocket, and contrasting lining. The contrast fabric and texture lends a very upscale look, but this bag would look equally fabulous in denim or a fabulous cotton print.

FINISHED SIZE:
9¼˝ wide × 11˝ tall × 3˝ deep

Supplies

Cotton yardage is based on 44˝-wide fabric.

FABRIC A: ½ yard of medium-weight to heavyweight cotton for bag exterior

FABRIC B: ⅝ yard of contrasting lightweight cotton fabric for lining

FABRIC C: ¼ yard of contrasting medium-weight to heavyweight cotton for side panel/gusset

FABRIC D: 1 piece at least 5˝ × 6˝ of medium-weight leather for pocket

INTERFACING: 1 yard

FUSIBLE FLEECE: ½ yard

COTTON WEBBING (1½˝ WIDE): 2 yards

BASIC SEWING TOOL KIT (page 24)

DENIM OR LEATHER SEWING MACHINE NEEDLE

PATTERN 8 (front and back; pullout page P2)

Cutting

FABRIC A

- Cut 2 from pattern 8.

FABRIC B

- Cut 2 from pattern 8.
- Cut 1 piece 4˝ × 32˝ for the gusset.

FABRIC C

- Cut 1 piece 4˝ × 30˝ for the gusset.

FABRIC D

- Trim the leather scrap to 5˝ × 6˝ for the pocket.

INTERFACING AND FUSIBLE FLEECE

- Cut 2 from pattern 8.
- Cut 2 pieces 3˝ × 20˝ for the gusset.

WEBBING STRAPS

- Cut 2 straps each 36˝ long.

Prepare

1. Trace pattern 8 and all the markings onto pattern paper. Cut out the paper pattern.

2. Fold fabric A in half with right sides together, and pin pattern 8 on the double layer of fabric.

3. Transfer the pattern markings to the fabric (page 19). Cut out the pieces.

4. Repeat Steps 2 and 3 to cut the same pieces from fabric B, interfacing, and fusible fleece.

5. Mark the cutting dimensions for the gusset on a single layer of fabric A, fabric B, interfacing, and fusible fleece. Cut them out.

6. Trim the 3˝ × 20˝ pieces to fit the strap and tab, placing them ½˝ from each end and overlapping ⅛˝. Fuse the interfacing and fleece to the wrong side of the exterior bag fabric. Refer to Applying Fusibles (page 33) for more information.

Make the Tote

All seams are sewn with a ½″ seam allowance unless otherwise noted.

1. Make the pocket. If using leather, make sure to use a leather needle in your machine and increase the stitch length to 3.5 mm.

2. Pin the pocket to the bag front, matching the markings. Edgestitch along the bottom edge (the side edges will be caught in the webbing). Backstitch at each end. *fig. A*

3. Pin webbing to the fabric A front, matching the markings. Align each end of the webbing just below the bottom edge, as shown. Pin it in place along the markings. Make sure the webbing isn't twisted. *fig. B*

4. Stitch the webbing in place along one inside edge, catching the edge of the pocket in the stitching. Stitch only as far up as the marking (you need to keep the webbing free near the top edge so you can finish the top edge of the bag). Pivot across the webbing at the top marking and down the other side. Backstitch. Repeat for the other side.

5. Pin and sew the second length of webbing to the fabric A back. You can add a pocket to the back, too, if you want.

6. Pin the fabric A front to the gusset, matching the markings. Use a lot of pins. Stitch slowly and smooth the fabric around the corners.

A

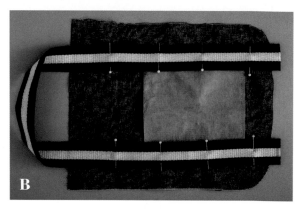

B

Tip

It helps to use lots of pins around curved seams to make stitching easier. I find that if I position the body side of the bag up and the gusset side down, I have more control over the evenness of the stitching and final shape of the bag.

7. Repeat to stitch the fabric A back to the other side of the gusset. Snip the thread ends and press. *fig. C*

8. Clip into the corner seam allowance to help form perfect corners on the finished bag. Trim the seam allowances. *fig. D*

9. Repeat Steps 6–8 with the fabric B pieces to make the lining; however, leave an opening in the stitching between the marked dots so you will be able to turn the bag right side out.

10. Insert the bag inside the lining with right sides together, and tuck the straps between the bag and lining. Pin around the top edge and stitch.

11. Turn the bag right side out; press and understitch the seam (page 52). *fig. E*

12. Tuck the raw edges of the opening inside the lining, press, and stitch the opening closed.

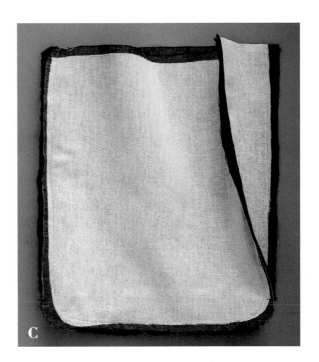

Making a Patch Pocket

1. Press all the edges of the pocket ¼″ toward the wrong side, except for the top edge. Use your pinking shears to cut along the top edge.

Tip

To make this easier, use ¼″-wide fusible tape around the left and right sides, as well as the bottom edge of the wrong side of the fabric. When you press the edges to the wrong side, the tape helps create a perfect ¼″ fold.

2. Fold and press the top edge 1″ toward the right side of the pocket. *fig. A*

3. Stitch just 1″ down from the top fold along each side. *fig. B*

4. Snip into the seam allowance so you can turn the top of the pocket right side out and have a nice, clean top edge. Push out the corners carefully.

5. Press and topstitch across the turned fold at the top of the pocket.

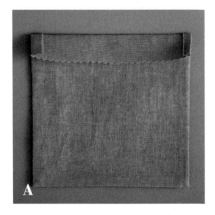

A

Tip

Some people prefer an inside pocket. You can follow the same directions but simply stitch it to the bag lining. If the bag isn't lined, the pocket stitching will show on the outside of the bag, so you might want to use colorful thread for a cool design feature.

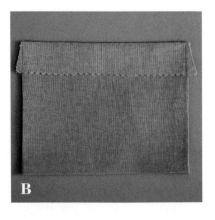

B

Abigail Boxed-Bottom Tote

This totally cool tote features a contrast bottom, a bright patch pocket, and bias-bound inside seams for a clean finished inside. There are endless opportunities to add your own signature touch!

FINISHED SIZE:
11˝ wide × 13¼˝ tall × 4˝ deep

Supplies

Cotton yardage is based on 44˝-wide fabric.

FABRIC A: 1 yard of medium-weight to heavyweight cotton for bag exterior

FABRIC B: ½ yard of kraft-tex for contrast bottom

FABRIC C: 6½˝ × 6½˝ square of cotton fabric for pocket

DOUBLE-FOLD BIAS TAPE (½˝ WIDE): 1 yard

BASIC SEWING TOOL KIT (page 24)

DENIM OR LEATHER SEWING MACHINE NEEDLE

WONDER CLIPS (Binder clips work, too!)

Cutting

FABRIC A

- Cut 1 piece 16˝ × 34˝ for the bag body.
- Cut 2 strap pieces 4˝ × 28˝.

FABRIC B

- Cut 1 piece 13˝ × 16˝.

Prepare

1. Mark the measurements for the bag front/back and straps on fabric A and cut out the pieces.

2. Mark the measurements for the bottom band on fabric B and cut out the piece.

Tip

kraft-tex is an exciting product by C&T Publishing. It functions like a paper-leather hybrid. Before using it on a real bag, I recommend playing with it first to get used to how it feels and behaves during stitching. To add strength and more leather-like texture, be sure to wash and dry it before cutting. I just crumple up my roll and toss it in the washer on a cold cycle with an old towel—no detergent necessary. Then put both the towel and the kraft-tex in the dryer to dry. Give it a good shake when you take it out of the dryer, press it flat, and get to cutting!

When sewing with kraft-tex, I do not use pins. Pins leave holes—instead, I prefer Wonder Clips. Also, I use a leather/denim sewing machine needle and increase the length of my stitch to 3.0 mm (a longer stitch.)

Make the Bag

All seams are sewn with a ½˝ seam allowance unless otherwise noted.

1. Center the bottom band over the bag front/back.

2. Topstitch on the right side, ¼˝ away from each long edge of the bottom band. *fig. A*

3. Make the patch pocket (page 74).

4. Center the pocket on the bag front. *fig. B*

5. Edgestitch the pocket to the bag front, ⅛˝ from the pressed edge. *fig. C*

6. Make 2 single-fold straps (refer to Making Straps, page 47). Add optional rows of stitching to the length of the straps; the stitching gives them a bit more strength.

7. Press the top edge of the bag front and back pieces ½˝ toward the wrong side and then again 1¼˝.

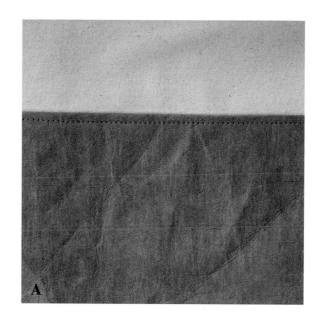

A

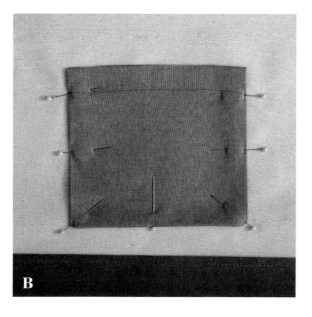

B

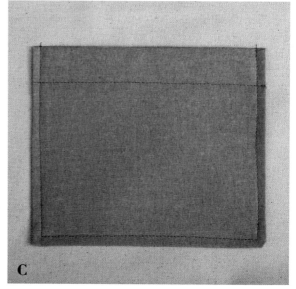

C

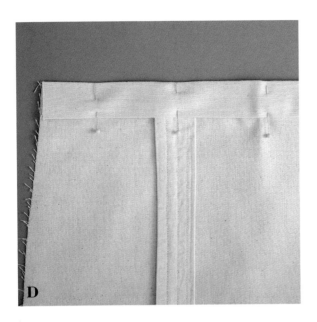

D

8. Position the ends of 1 strap on the bag front by sliding the ends of the strap under the top folded edge. Make sure the strap is not twisted and pin the strap ends in place. *fig. D*

9. Machine stitch ¼″ from the bottom folded edge along the top of the bag front, catching the strap in the stitching.

10. Flip the strap upward, press, and pin them in place. *fig. E*

11. Topstitch across the top of the bag, catching the strap in the stitching. *fig. F*

12. Repeat Steps 7–11 for the bag back.

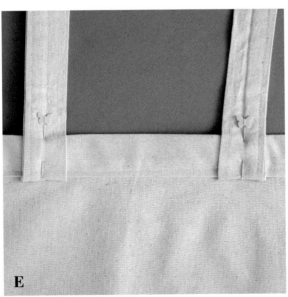

E

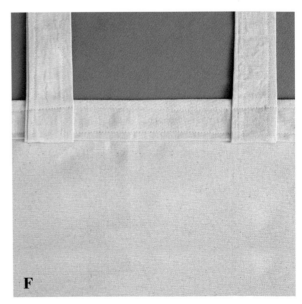

F

Put It All Together

1. Fold the bottom band in half so the right sides of the bag front and back align and the top edges of the bottom band align on each side seam.

2. Pin the fabric and use clips at the kraft-tex to secure the side seams.

3. Stitch each side seam with a ½˝ seam allowance. Backstitch and snip the thread ends.

4. Refer to Making a Flat Bottom with Boxed Corners, Method 2 (page 69).

5. Turn your bag right side out. Using your hands, shape the bottom. kraft-tex can be a bit stiff to turn out. Take your time, and it will look great!

6. For a bag that is just as cute on the inside, bind the inside seam allowances with bias tape. Trim the seam allowances so they are even. *fig. A*

7. Unfold the bias tape. With right sides together and the raw edges even, pin (or clip) the bias tape to the fabric. Refer to Binding a Fabric Edge with Bias Tape (page 80). *figs. B & C*

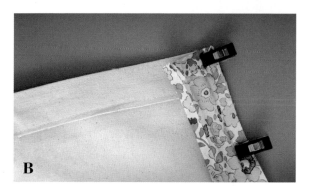

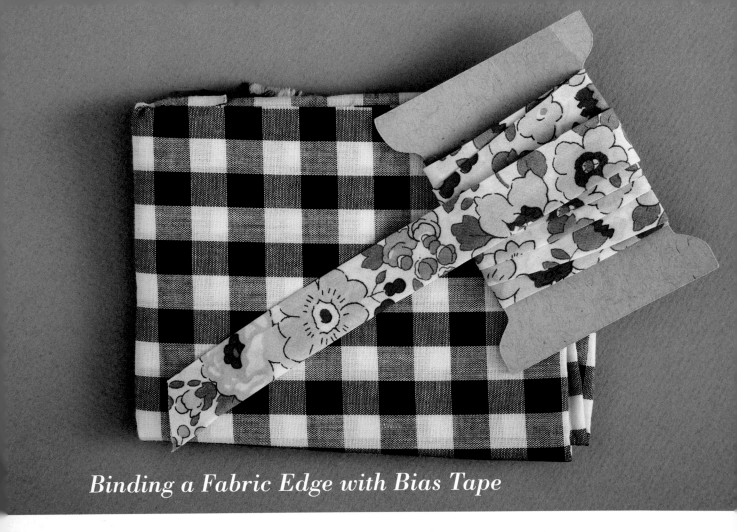

Binding a Fabric Edge with Bias Tape

Bias binding is a lovely way to finish a curved or straight edge of a bag. You can buy precut and folded bias tape in an amazing variety of colors and patterns, or you can make your own bias binding from fabric by cutting bias strips from yardage and then joining them to obtain the necessary length.

The following instructions demonstrate how to attach ½″-wide double-fold bias tape to a fabric edge.

1. Unfold the bias tape. With right sides together, pin the bias tape to the fabric with the raw edges even. Stitch these together with a ½″ seam allowance. *fig. A*

Tip

Use the fold of the bias tape as a stitching guide.

2. Press the bias tape up and over the seam. *fig. B*

3. Trim the seam allowance. *fig. C*

4. Fold the bias tape over the raw edge of the fabric and press. *fig. D*

5. Pin the loose edge of the bias tape in place to encase the seam allowance. *fig. E*

6. Edgestitch the bias tape in place along the folded edge. *fig. F*

Zipper Clutches

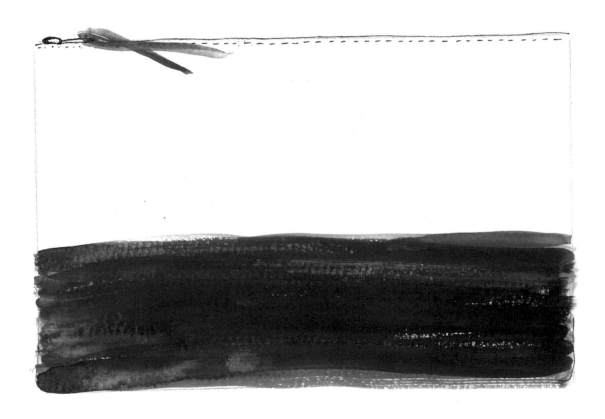

Hollis Lined Clutch

This simple little clutch has a zipper closing to keep all your special things safe.
It is lined for extra durability and to hide all those raveling seam allowances!

FINISHED SIZE:
10½˝ wide × 9˝ tall

Supplies

Cotton yardage is based on 44˝-wide fabric.

FABRIC A: ½ yard of medium-weight to heavyweight cotton for bag exterior

FABRIC B: ½ yard of contrasting lightweight cotton for lining

INTERFACING: ½ yard

1 METAL-TEETH ZIPPER (10˝ LONG)

BASIC SEWING TOOL KIT (page 24)

Cutting

FABRIC A

- Cut 2, each 11½˝ × 10˝.

FABRIC B

- Cut 2, each 11½˝ × 10˝.

INTERFACING

- Cut 2, each 10½˝ × 9˝.

Prepare

1. Cut fabric A, fabric B, and the interfacing as indicated in the cutting instructions.

2. Fuse the interfacing to the wrong side of the fabric A pieces. If your fabric still needs a bit more structure, add a layer of fleece directly over the interfacing. Refer to Applying Fusibles (page 33) for more information.

Make the Clutch

All seams are sewn with a ½˝ seam allowance unless otherwise noted.

1. Install the zipper between the clutch front and back fabric A pieces along the 11½˝ side. Refer to Install an Exposed Zipper in the Top of a Bag (page 87). Because the clutch is lined, stitch the zipper to the fabric ¼˝ from the zipper teeth.

2. Pin one of the fabric B pieces on top of the fabric A piece, with the zipper sandwiched between, right sides together, and the raw edges aligned. Stitch ¼˝ from the edge of the fabric. *fig. A*

3. Open the lining and press it away from the zipper. Topstitch close to the folded edge through the lining, zipper, and fabric A.

4. Repeat Steps 2 and 3 to stitch the remaining fabric B piece to the other side of the zipper. *fig. B*

Put It All Together

1. This next step is important! You'll need to switch back to the standard presser foot. Unzip about one-third of the zipper, otherwise it will be difficult to unzip once the clutch is sewn.

2. Pin the front and back of the exterior fabric pieces with right sides together, and pin the front and back lining pieces with right sides together, as shown. Sew around the perimeter of the bag with a ½″ seam allowance, starting and stopping at the marked openings. Be sure to reverse stitch. *fig. C*

3. Trim the corners diagonally to reduce bulk. Press.

4. Turn the clutch right side out. Reach into the opening of the lining and use your fingers to push out the corners of the bag.

5. Give the lining a good press, and press the seam allowances of the opening to the inside. Hand or machine stitch the opening closed. Tuck the lining into the bag and press it a final time.

C

Tip

Dress up your clutch with fancy fabric, silk lining, and a piece of 1½″-wide grosgrain ribbon tied to the zipper pull.

All About Zippers

No need to feel intimidated by zippers—I'm happy to teach you some insertion tricks and techniques. You will feel so accomplished once you master the zipper!

There are three types of zippers, and they all have twill tape attached to molded plastic teeth, polyester interlocking coil teeth, or metal teeth. I prefer metal-teeth zippers.

Tip

I really like YKK zippers because the twill tape has two stitching guidelines down each side of the zipper teeth. You'll have to look carefully to see them! One is ⅛″ from the teeth, and the other is ¼″ from the teeth. Depending on much of the twill tape you want visible in the finished bag, you can sew on either guideline. When the bag is lined, it is usually best to sew on the ¼″ guideline so the lining doesn't get caught in the zipper.

- You will need a zipper foot (most sewing machines come with one).

- Inserting a zipper takes practice. When I am learning a new technique, I like to practice on scrap fabric to build up my confidence. Practice with different types of zippers and different insertion methods.

- Metal zippers are tricky to shorten. Best to purchase the correct length.

- If the zipper tape doesn't have stitching guidelines, measure ⅛″ or ¼″ from the edge of the zipper teeth and mark your own stitching guideline on the zipper tape with tailor's chalk.

- I always hand baste a zipper to the fabric before sewing it in place. You can use pins instead of basting, but when I do, the zipper never goes in straight. If you baste with brightly colored thread, it is easy to see the basting stitches and easy to remove them once the zipper is in place.

- Sometimes stitching around the zipper pull can be a bit tricky. Before you begin stitching, unzip about one-third of the zipper and sew to that point. Then, with the needle in the down position, lift the presser foot so you can wiggle the zipper pull up to close the zipper; resume sewing.

Shortening a Zipper

Zippers are available at most fabric stores in a variety of lengths, ranging from 7″ to 22″. However, there may be times when you would like to shorten a zipper. Maybe the color that you want is not available in the exact size that you need for your project. Zippers can be easily shortened! Especially ones with nylon or coil teeth.

The length of a zipper is measured from the top stop to the bottom zipper stop—not the actual top to bottom of the tape. Using a ruler or seam gauge, measure and mark on the zipper tape where the new zipper stop should be placed.

To make a new stop, you are going to create a bar tack. This can be done using you sewing machine's bar-tack function or zigzag stitch or by hand stitching over the coils a few times. Whichever method you choose, you will stitch through the zipper tape and around the coils, wrapping them tightly to create a new stop.

Once you have sewn the bar tack, simply use an old pair of standard scissors and cut the remaining length of the zipper about ½″ beyond the bar tack. Your zipper is ready to use!

Install an Exposed Zipper in the Top of a Bag

Choose a zipper that is 1″ shorter than the opening in the top of the bag so there will be ½″ of fabric beyond the length of zipper at each end. Seam allowances are ½″ unless otherwise noted.

1. Install the zipper foot on your sewing machine.

2. Lay out the 2 pieces of fabric that will joined by the zipper. Press the seam allowances of the zipper seam to the wrong side so you can use the pressed folds as guidelines. You might want to pink the raw edges if the fabric ravels.

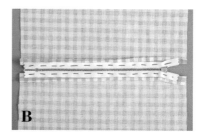

3. Open the pressed fold of one of the pieces. Hand baste one side of the zipper facedown to the right side of the fabric so that the zipper teeth will extend slightly beyond the pressed fold. *fig. A*

4. Close the zipper and repeat Step 3 to baste the other side of the zipper to the remaining piece of fabric. *fig. B*

5. With the fabric right side up, machine stitch one side of the zipper, ⅛″ or ¼″ from the zipper teeth, beginning and ending with a backstitch. *fig. C*

6. Press the stitching, taking care not to press the zipper teeth (especially if the teeth are plastic).

7. Repeat Steps 5 and 6 to stitch the opposite side of the zipper in place.

Gracie Lined Pouch

*If you want your clutch to stand flat, all you need to do is make
a boxed bottom (see Making a Boxed Bottom, Method 2, page 69).
If you want your boxed bottom clutch lined, follow these steps.*

FINISHED SIZE:
10˝ wide × 5˝ tall × 3˝ deep

Supplies

Cotton yardage is based on 44˝-wide fabric.

FABRIC A: ⅜ yard of medium-weight to heavyweight cotton for bag exterior

FABRIC B: ⅜ yard of contrasting lightweight cotton for lining

INTERFACING: ⅜ yard

1 METAL-TEETH ZIPPER (10˝ LONG)

BASIC SEWING TOOL KIT (page 24)

Cutting

FABRIC A

- Cut 2, each 8˝ × 11˝.

FABRIC B

- Cut 2, each 8˝ × 11˝.

INTERFACING

- Cut 2, each 7˝ × 10˝.

Prepare

1. Cut fabric A, fabric B, and the interfacing as indicated in the cutting instructions.

2. Fuse the interfacing to the wrong side of the fabric A pieces. If your fabric still needs a bit more structure, add a layer of fleece directly over the interfacing. Refer to Applying Fusibles (page 33) for more information.

Make the Pouch

All seams are sewn with a ½˝ seam allowance unless otherwise noted.

1. Follow the instructions for installing the zipper (see Install an Exposed Zipper in the Top of a Bag, page 87).

2. Follow the instructions for how to line a clutch with an exposed zipper (Hollis Lined Clutch, Make the Clutch, Steps 2–4, page 84).

3. You'll need to switch to standard presser foot now. Unzip about one-third of the zipper, otherwise it will be difficult to unzip once the clutch is sewn.

4. Pin the front and back of the fabric A pieces with right sides together and the front and back fabric B pieces with right sides together. *fig. A*

5. Stitch around the perimeter of the bag with a ½˝ seam allowance, starting and stopping at the markings in the lining. Backstitch. Snip the thread ends and press.

6. Use a transparent ruler and tailor's chalk or a water-soluble pen to mark a 1½˝ square on each bottom corner of the exterior and lining pieces (see Making a Flat Bottom with Boxed Corners, Method 1, page 68).

7. Turn the bag right side out, tuck the lining into the bag, and shape the corners to form the flat bottom.

8. Fold the seam allowances in the opening of the lining to the inside. Hand or machine stitch the lining closed; press.

Harley Wristlet

Look what adding a strap does to this little clutch! Now you can carry it on your wrist and keep your hands free.

FINISHED SIZE:
10˝ wide × 6½˝ tall

Supplies

Cotton yardage is based on 44˝-wide fabric.

FABRIC A: ⅜ yard of medium-weight to heavyweight cotton for bag exterior and strap

FABRIC B: ⅜ yard of contrasting lightweight cotton for lining and strap

INTERFACING: ⅜ yard

1 METAL-TEETH ZIPPER (10˝ LONG)

1 D-RING (½˝ WIDE)

1 SWIVEL SNAP HOOK (½˝ WIDE)

BASIC SEWING TOOL KIT (page 24)

Cutting

FABRIC A

- Cut 2 for the bag front and back, each 7½˝ × 11˝.

- Cut 1 strap 2˝ × 18˝.

FABRIC B

- Cut 2 for the lining, each 7½˝ × 11˝.

INTERFACING

- Cut 2 for the bag front and back, each 6½˝ × 10˝.

Prepare

1. Cut fabric A, fabric B, and the interfacing as indicated in the cutting instructions.

2. Fuse the interfacing to the wrong side of the fabric A pieces. If your fabric still needs a bit more structure, add a layer of fleece directly over the interfacing. Refer to Applying Fusibles (page 33) for more information.

Make the Strap and Tabs

1. Make the single-fold strap (refer to Making Straps, page 47), except sew across one short end before turning right side out.

2. From the open end of the finished strap, cut 1 piece 3″ long for the tab.

3. Fold the tab end through the D-ring and stitch the raw edges together. Fold the strap through the swivel hook and baste the ends together about 1½″ from the edges. *fig. A*

4. Trim the open end of the strap close to the stitching. Fold the closed end over and stitch through all 3 layers, close to the swivel hook. *fig. B*

Put It All Together

1. Baste the ends of the tab to the right side of 1 fabric A piece, as marked on the pattern.

2. Follow the instructions for installing a zipper in a lined clutch (see Install an Exposed Zipper in the Top of a Bag, page 87).

3. Unzip about one-third of the zipper, otherwise it will be difficult to unzip once the clutch is sewn. Switch to the standard presser foot.

4. Pin the front and back fabric A pieces with right sides together (with the tab end and strap sandwiched between them) and the front and back fabric B with right sides together. See Hollis Lined Clutch, Put It All Together (page 85).

5. Stitch around the perimeter of the bag with a ½˝ seam allowance, starting and stopping at one side of the lining and leaving a 3˝ opening for turning; backstitch. Snip the thread ends and press.

6. Trim the corners diagonally to reduce bulk and press.

7. Turn the clutch right side out. Reach in the opening of the lining and use your fingers to push out the corners of the bag.

8. Give the lining a good press, and press the seam allowances of the opening to the inside. Hand or machine stitch the opening closed. Tuck the lining into the bag and press it a final time.

Tip

Dress up the clutch with a band of frayed fabric!

Make your own decorative trim with a narrow strip of fabric. Use a seam ripper, tweezers, or even your fingers to tease out a few parallel threads. Gently pull the thread from one side to the other. When you are pleased with the width, press the strip and then stitch it place. The stitching will prevent the strip from unraveling anymore.

Practice on a variety of fabrics and experiment by cutting on various grainlines. You can even layer fabric, fringe, and ribbon trims. Work some magic!

Drawstring Bags

Rachel Drawstring Pouch

It's time to make a super-easy and super-cute drawstring bag! With a secure drawstring closure to cinch off the top of this pouch, it works as well for daytime and on evenings out. This style is made with space for your essentials, such as your keys, cards, lipstick, and phone.

FINISHED SIZE:
11″ wide × 7″ tall × 3″ deep

Rachel Low — Girl's Guide to DIY Fashion — FunStitch STUDIO

Sue Kim — Boutique Bags — stash BOOKS

ANNABEL WRIGLEY — We Love to Sew—Gifts — FunStitch STUDIO

Supplies

Cotton and silk yardage is based on 44˝-wide fabric.

FABRIC A: ½ yard of medium-weight cotton or silk for bag exterior

FABRIC B: ½ yard of medium-weight cotton or silk for lining

CORDING (¼˝ OR ½˝ DIAMETER): 1 yard

BASIC SEWING TOOL KIT (page 24)

SAFETY PIN OR BODKIN

PATTERN 9 (front and back; pullout page P1)

Cutting

FABRIC A

- Cut 2 using pattern 9.

FABRIC B

- Cut 2 using pattern 9.

CORDING

- Cut 2 pieces 18˝ long.

Prepare

1. Trace the front/back pattern piece and all the markings onto paper. Cut out the paper pattern. Fold each selvage of the fabric toward the center of the fabric, right sides together. Either trace the pattern 2 times *or* pin it once, cut it out, and then pin it again to the double layer of fabrics A and B. Pin so the pattern fold line is positioned along the fabric fold.

2. Transfer the pattern markings to the fabric (page 19). Cut out the fabric around the outside pattern lines.

Make the Pouch

All seams are sewn with a ½˝ seam allowance unless otherwise noted.

Note

A casing creates a finished opening for the drawstring. There are a lot of different ways to make a casing, but for this project, the casing is formed between the outside fabric and the lining.

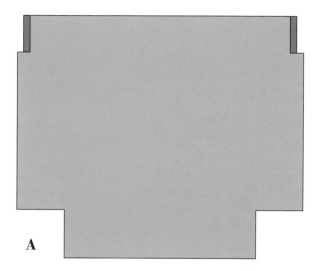

A

1. Clip into the seam allowance at the marking near the top edge of the bag, as shown. Press the seam allowance above the clips to the wrong side. Do this for both the bag front and back and both lining pieces. *fig. A*

2. With right sides together, stitch the top edge of the bag front to the top edge of 1 lining piece. Repeat for the remaining bag piece and the lining pieces. Press. Understitch the lining (page 52).

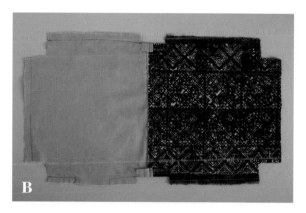

B

3. With right sides together, pin the bag front and back together along the sides and bottom edges and the lining the same way. Start stitching just below the folded seam allowances at the top edges of the bag exterior and the lining, as shown. Leave an opening in one side of the lining so you can turn the pouch right side out later. *fig. B*

4. Snip the thread ends and press.

5. To form the boxed bottom of the bag, see Making a Boxed Bottom, Method 1 (page 68). Repeat for the lining.

6. Turn the bag right side out through the opening in the lining. Smooth the lining inside the bag so the wrong sides are together. Press. Pin the top edges together. Topstitch the bag and lining together ¾˝ from the top edge to create the casing for the cording. *fig. C*

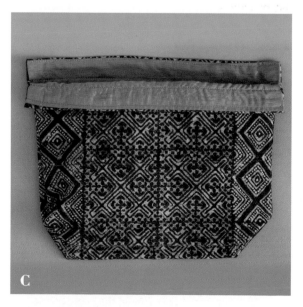

C

Feed the Cord

1. Use a safety pin or bodkin to feed 1 piece of cording through the casing on one side of the bag and then through the opposite casing. *fig. D*

2. Feed the remaining piece of cording through the casings in the opposite direction. *fig. E*

3. Even out the cords and knot the ends of the draw-strings together at each side.

Bunny Backpack

This soft, synthetic microfiber suede drawstring bag is an
upgrade from the pack of your school days!

FINISHED SIZE:
11˝ wide × 15½˝ tall × 3˝ deep

Supplies

Cotton yardage is based on 44˝-wide fabric.

FABRIC A: 2 yards of medium-weight cotton or heavyweight flannel *or* 1 yard of 60˝-wide synthetic microfiber suede for bag exterior

INTERFACING: ½ yard (if using cotton fabric)

BASIC SEWING TOOL KIT (page 24)

SEWING MACHINE NEEDLE SIZE 9 OR 11

PATTERNS 10 AND 11 (front and back, and flap; pullout page P2)

Cutting

FABRIC A

- Cut 2 each from patterns 10 and 11.

- Cut 2 straps, each 2½˝ × 60˝.

INTERFACING (FLAP):

- Cut 1 from pattern 11.

Prepare

1. Trace the front/back pattern, the flap pattern, and all the markings onto paper. Cut out 1 or 2 paper patterns. You need to cut each of the patterns 2 times from folded fabric.

2. On a single layer of fabric A, use the strap measurements and tailor's chalk or a fabric-marking pen to measure and mark the strap dimensions onto the fabric. Cut out the strap.

3. Fold each selvage of the fabric toward the center of the fabric, right sides together. Pin

pattern pieces 10 and 11 on a double layer of fabric, with the pattern fold lines positioned along the fabric fold.

4. Transfer the pattern markings to the fabric (page 19). Cut out the fabric around the outside pattern lines.

5. For cotton fabric, fuse the interfacing to the wrong side of 1 flap piece. Refer to Applying Fusibles (page 33) for more information.

Make the Backpack

All seams are sewn with a ½" seam allowance unless otherwise noted. Adjust your stitch length to 10–12 stitches per inch if using synthetic microfiber suede.

1. Make 2 double-fold drawstring straps (page 47).

2. Cut 1 piece 4" long from each of the finished straps for the tabs. Set them aside.

3. Clip into the seam allowance at the marking near the top edge of the bag, as shown. Press the seam allowance above the clips to the wrong side. Do this for both the bag front and back.

4. Press the top edge to the wrong side and stitch along the pattern markings to form the casing on the front and back pieces.

5. Pin the ends of the 2 tabs to the right side of the bag front at the pattern markings. Baste them in place.

6. With right sides together, pin the bag front and back together along the sides and bottom edges. Start stitching just below the finished extensions (at the marked channel stitching line) and backstitch. Do not stitch the finished extensions together. Include the tab ends in the stitching.

7. Snip the thread ends and press.

8. Use a transparent ruler and tailor's chalk or a water-soluble pen to mark a 1½" × 1½" square on the bottom corners of the front and back pieces. See Making a Flat Bottom with Boxed Corners, Method 1 (page 68).

Make and Attach the Flap

1. Pin the flap pieces with right sides together. Stitch all but the top edge. Trim the seam allowance and press.

2. Turn the flap right side out and press.

3. If you want, topstitch close to the finished edge of the flap. Stitch slowly and carefully—these stitches are decorative. This is your time to shine!

4. Pin the flap to the upper edge of the bag front, with the top edge of the flap just above the channel stitching line. Stitch across the top of the flap with a ¼″ seam allowance. *fig. A*

5. Flip the flap up, press, and topstitch ¼″ from the seam. This holds the flap in place and hides the seam allowance. *fig. B*

Feed the Drawstrings

1. Use a safety pin or bodkin to feed the drawstrings through the channels (see Feed the Cord, page 100).

2. On each side, thread the 2 drawstrings down through the tabs and knot each one separately. *fig. C*

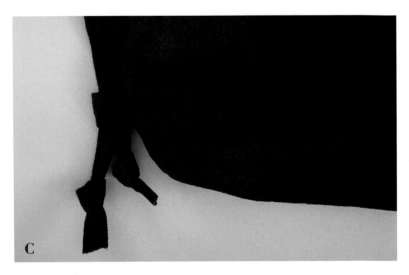

Swayze Cinch Bag with Grommets

Luxurious fabric, leather tassels, metallic grommets, and decorative embellishments turn this drawstring bag into an evening or special occasion bag. There is so much you can do to add your own special touch and make this super-simple bag spectacular!

FINISHED SIZE:
14˝ wide × 16½˝ tall

Supplies

Cotton yardage is based on 44˝-wide fabric.

FABRIC A: ¾ yard of medium-weight cotton or synthetic microfiber suede for bag exterior

INTERFACING: 5˝ × 15˝ scrap (*optional*)

CORDING: 3½ yards (I used Paracord size 550 [⁵⁄₃₂˝ diameter].)

GROMMETS: 2 or 4 (Remember: You are the designer!)

GROMMET SETTING KIT

MALLET

SEW-ON OR FUSIBLE DECORATIVE FLOWERS OR TRIMS (*optional*)

BASIC SEWING TOOL KIT (page 24)

SAFETY PIN OR BODKIN

PATTERNS 10 AND 12 (front and back, and grommet placement; pullout pages P1 and P2)

Cutting

FABRIC A

- Cut 2 using pattern 10.

CORDING

- Cut 2 pieces 63˝ long.

INTERFACING

- Cut 1 using pattern 12.

Prepare

1. Trace the front/back pattern piece and all the markings onto paper. Cut out the paper pattern.

2. Fold the fabric in half, right sides together, and pin the pattern piece along the fabric fold. Cut 2: 1 for the bag front and 1 for the bag back.

3. Transfer the pattern markings to the fabric (page 19). Cut out the fabric. Use pattern 12 (the grommet placement guide) to mark the grommet locations and to mark placement for interfacing if you choose to interface the grommet area.

4. If desired, cut 2 pieces of interfacing using pattern 12 (the grommet placement guide). Apply the interfacing to the wrong side of the bag front and back along the bottom edge of the both the front and back fabric pieces. The interfacing helps support the grommets.

Make the Cinch Bag

All seams are sewn with a ½˝ seam allowance unless otherwise noted.

1. Clip into the seam allowance at the marking near the top edge of the bag, as shown. Press the seam allowance above the clips to the wrong side. Do this for both the bag front and back and both lining pieces.

2. Press the top edge of both the front and back to the wrong side along the marked fold line. *fig. A*

3. Stitch along the marked stitching line to form the casing on the front and back pieces.

4. With right sides together, pin the bag front and back together along the sides and bottom edges. Start stitching just below the finished extensions (at the marked channel stitching line) and backstitch. Do not stitch the finished extensions together.

5. Snip the thread ends and press.

6. Turn the bag right side out.

7. Stitch through both layers 2˝ above the bottom of the bag, along the marked line. *fig. B*

8. Insert the grommets in the marked location (see Setting Grommets, page 109).

C

Feed the Cord

1. Use a safety pin or bodkin to feed 1 piece of cording through the inside grommet on one side of the bag. Go up through the casing on the bag front and bag back and then down and through the outside grommet on the same side of the bag. Leave lengths of cording at each end.

2. Repeat with the remaining piece of cording through the grommets on the other side of the bag, threading the cord in the opposite direction through the casing.

3. Knot the ends of the cording together at the bottom of bag, or make and add tassels to the ends of the cording (see Leather Tassels, page 38). *fig. C*

4. Add embellishments as desired!

Setting Grommets

1. Cut a very small hole or an *X* in the center of the marked hole to help the grommet pierce the fabric. Be careful—if the hole is too large, the grommet will fall through. You can use the tips of sharp scissors or a craft knife. *fig. A*

2. Insert the grommet from the right side into the cut hole so it pushes through to the bag back (through the interfacing).

3. Place the washer over the grommet sticking out through the hole. *fig. B*

4. Move to a sturdy work surface. Place the anvil under the *front* of your grommet and place the setter on top (on top of the *back* of your grommet). Give the setter a few good whacks with the mallet.

What's Next?

Congratulations! I hope that you found some valuable sewing advice and lessons in this book, and I encourage you to keep practicing. The skills you have gained are infinitely adaptable in the development of your own designs. Trick-or-treat bags, holiday baskets, and sports totes are all simple bags! With a little ingenuity, passion, and elbow grease, there is no limit to your potential.

Here are some of the things that inspire me.

Fabric stores: Purl Soho, Hawthorne Supply Co., Liberty London, Spoonflower

Fashion sites: Instagram, Net-a-Porter, Collette, The Sartorialist

Fashion history books: *Seeing Through Clothes*, by Anne Hollander; *D.V.*, by Diana Vreeland; *Chanel: A Woman of Her Own*, by Axel Madsen; *Claire McCardell Redefining Modernism*, by Kohle Yohannan; *100 Dresses*, by Harold Koda

Sewing books: *We Love to Sew* series, by Annabel Wrigley (C&T Publishing); *Sewing School*, by Amie Petronis Plumley and Andria Lisle; *Girl's Guide to DIY Fashion*, by Rachel Low (C&T Publishing); *I Had a Favorite Dress*, by Boni Ashburn; *Coco Chanel*, by Ma Isabel Sánchez Vegara; *Crafty Chloe*, by Kelly DiPucchio; *Main Street*, by Ann M. Martin; *How to be a Fashion Designer*, by Lesley Ware; *Sew Fab: Sewing and Style for Young Fashionistas*, by Lesley Ware

About the Author

Hilarie Wakefield Dayton is the owner of Little Stitch Studio (Norfolk, Virginia), where children can connect with each other, discover new things, and create something beautiful. She teaches weekly classes as well as camps and workshops. Little Stitch Studio is the perfect place for little designers to get inspired.

Visit Hilarie online and follow on social media!

Website
littlestitchstudionorfolk.com

Facebook
/littlestitchstudionorfolk

Pinterest
/hwdayton

Instagram
@littlestitchstudio

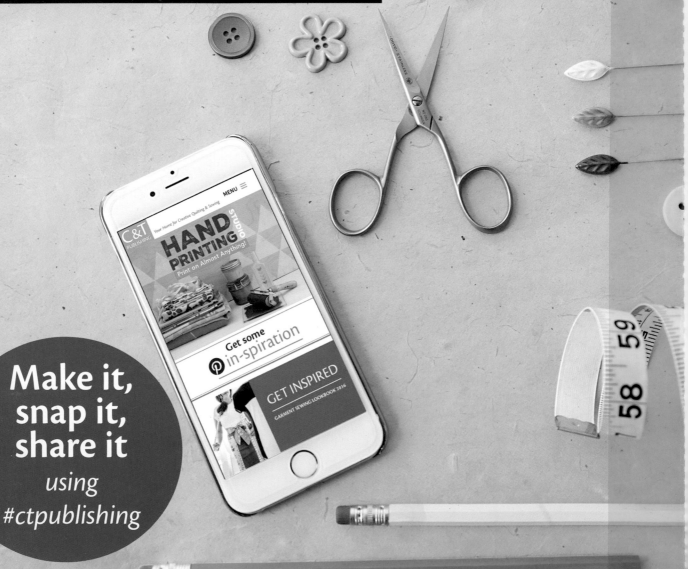

Want even more creative content?

Make it, snap it, share it *using* *#ctpublishing*